ESSENTIAL ELEMENTS for Band

COMPREHENSIVE BAND METHOD

TIM LAUTZENHEISER • JOHN HIGGINS • CHARLES MENGHINI
PAUL LAVENDER • TOM C. RHODES • DON BIERSCHENK

Percussion consultant and editor
WILL RAPP

To create an account, visit:
www.essentialelementsinteractive.com

Student Activation Code
E2PC-2781-7928-8928

ISBN 979-835013691-3

REVIEW

KEY SIGNATURE 
Key of B♭

TIME SIGNATURES
4/4 2/4

NOTES / RESTS: Whole, Half, Quarter, Eighths, Sixteenths

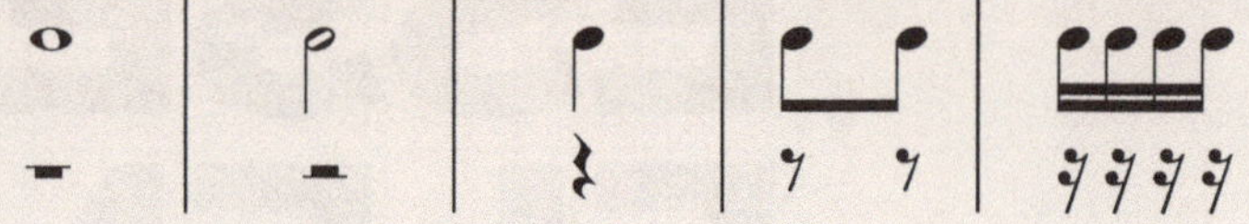

REPEAT SIGN

TEMPO MARKINGS
Allegro
Moderato

TIE

Pitched Percussion
(Keyboards and Timpani)

Other Percussion
(S.D., B.D., Tamb., Cym., etc.)
S.D.
B.D.

DYNAMICS
p - *mf* - *f*

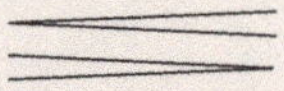

PERCUSSION REVIEW

MULTIPLE BOUNCE

CLOSED ROLL

SUSPENDED CYMBAL

EXTENDED ROLL

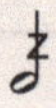

RUDIMENT
Flam

1. TECHNIQUE TRAX

2. WELCOME SONG

African Folk Song

Allegro

mf

3. THAILAND LULLABY

Thai Folk Song

Moderato
Snares off
S.D.
B.D.
Sus. Cym.
p
p
p

PERCUSSION REVIEW
ONE MEASURE REPEAT
SUSPENDED CYMBAL WITH STICK
TAMBOURINE
COWBELL
4. SHEPHERD'S HEY
English Folk Song
Moderato
S.D.
B.D.
Tamb.
5. THE CRAWDAD SONG
American Folk Song
Allegro
S.D.
B.D.
Sus. Cym. with Stick
Cowbell
4
8
12

REVIEW

KEY SIGNATURES

Key of E♭  Key of F

TIME SIGNATURES

$\frac{3}{4}$ C

Dotted Half Note

Dotted Quarter & Eighth Notes

1st & 2nd ENDINGS

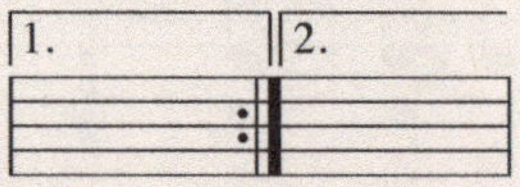

1. 2.

PICK-UP NOTES

TEMPO MARKINGS

Andante
Maestoso

PERCUSSION REVIEW

CLOSED ROLL

TRIANGLE

SLEIGH BELLS

RUDIMENT

Flam Accent

L R L R R L R L

6. AMERICA/GOD SAVE THE QUEEN

Based on a Traditional Anthem

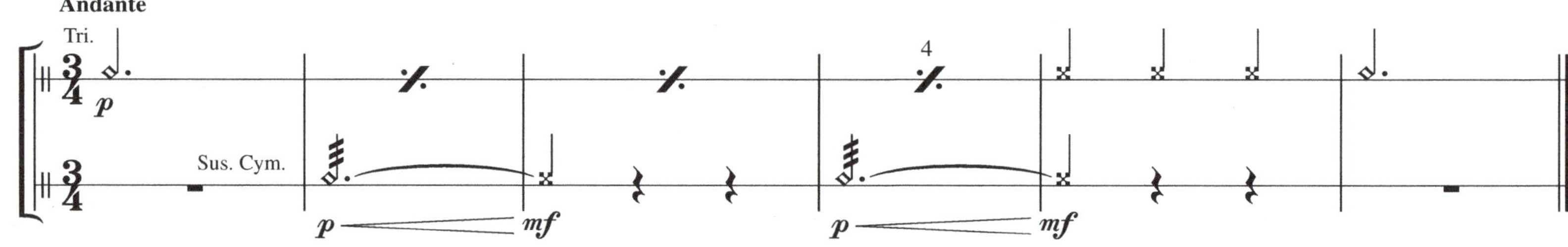

7. WEARING OF THE GREEN

Irish Folk Song

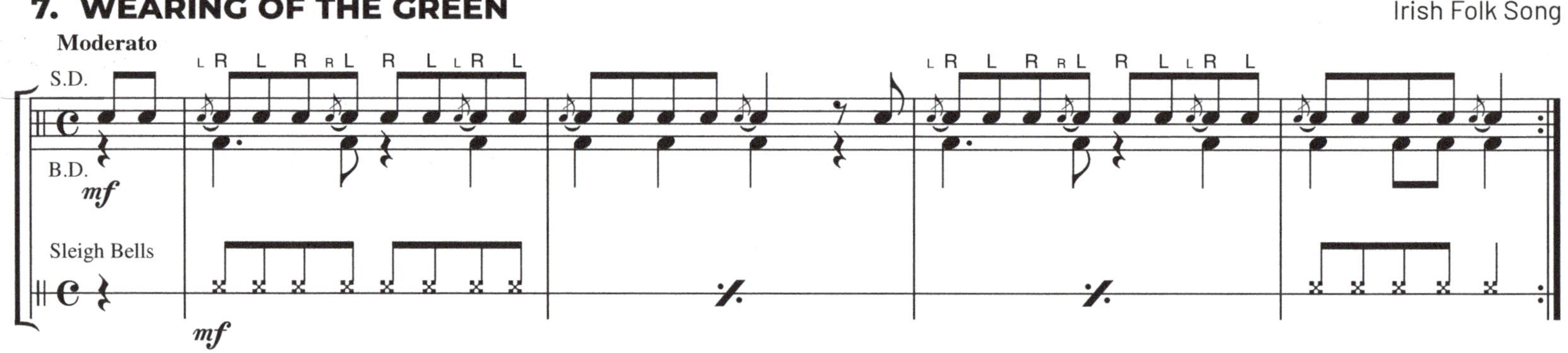

8. ROSES FROM THE SOUTH

Johann Strauss, Jr.

PERCUSSION REVIEW

CRASH CYMBAL | TIMPANI | TIMPANI ROLL | MULTIPLE MEASURE REST 2 | ACCENT >

8. ROSES FROM THE SOUTH – Timpani

Tune to F and C

9. CRUISIN' THROUGH THE PARK

10. TRUMPET VOLUNTARY – Duet

Jeremiah Clarke

10. TRUMPET VOLUNTARY – Timpani

Tune to B♭ and E♭

REVIEW
MULTIPLE MEASURE REST
2
ACCENT
FERMATA
D.C. al FINE
Eighth Note & Eighth Rest
Eighth Rest & Eighth Note
Eighth Note & Dotted Quarter Note
PERCUSSION REVIEW
RUDIMENT
Paradiddle
Double Paradiddle
Triple Paradiddle
RIM SHOT
R.S.
MARACAS
CLAVES
WOOD BLOCK
DOUBLE STICKING
DOUBLING
11. CHROMA-ZONE
mf
Fine
D.C. al Fine
f
12. BILLY BOY
American Folk Song
Moderato
S.D.
B.D.
f
Wood Block
f
mf
f

13. TECHNIQUE TRAX

14. SALSA SIESTA – Duet

Temple Blocks

See inside front cover for information on accessing instructional videos.

Temple Blocks (or Chinese Wood Blocks) include five different size blocks usually mounted on a stand. The hollow sounding blocks of different pitches create a distinctive and effective sound in a percussion section. For the best sound, use a soft to medium rubber mallet and play toward the edge of the top surface near the side with the open slit.

15. TREADING LIGHTLY

16. SMOOTH MOVE

17. SHIFTING GEARS

English composer **Thomas Tallis** (1508–1585) served as a royal court composer for Kings Henry VIII and Edward VI, and Queens Mary and Elizabeth. During Tallis' lifetime, the artist Michelangelo painted the Sistine Chapel.

Canons (one or more parts imitating the first part) were used in many forms by 16th century composers. A **Round** is a strict (or exact) canon which can be repeated any number of times without stopping. Play *Tallis Canon* as a 4-part round.

HISTORY

18. TALLIS CANON – Round (for Brass and W.W.)

Thomas Tallis

Percussion: If your band does *not* perform this exercises as a round, skip the 1st ending and the repeat.

Sightreading

Sightreading means playing a musical piece for the first time. The key to sightreading success is to know what to look for *before* you play. Use the word **S-T-A-R-S** to remind yourself what to look for, and eventually your band will become sightreading STARS!

S – **Sharps or flats** in the key signature
T – **Time signature** and **tempo markings**
A – **Accidentals** not found in the key signature
R – **Rhythms**, silently counting the more difficult notes and rests
S – **Signs**, including dynamics, articulations, repeats and endings

19. SIGHTREADING CHALLENGE

DAILY WARM-UPS

WORK-OUTS FOR TONE & TECHNIQUE

20. TONE BUILDER

21. FLEXIBILITY STUDY

22. TECHNIQUE TRAX *Practice Paradiddles as marked.*

23. CHORALE

Johann Sebastian Bach

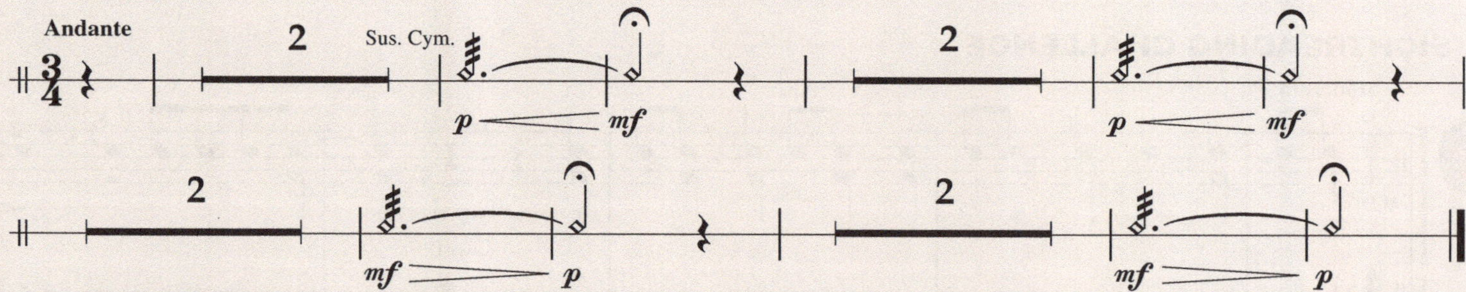

23. CHORALE – Timpani

Johann Sebastian Bach

Tune to B♭ and E♭

24. GRANDFATHER'S CLOCK

Henry C. Work

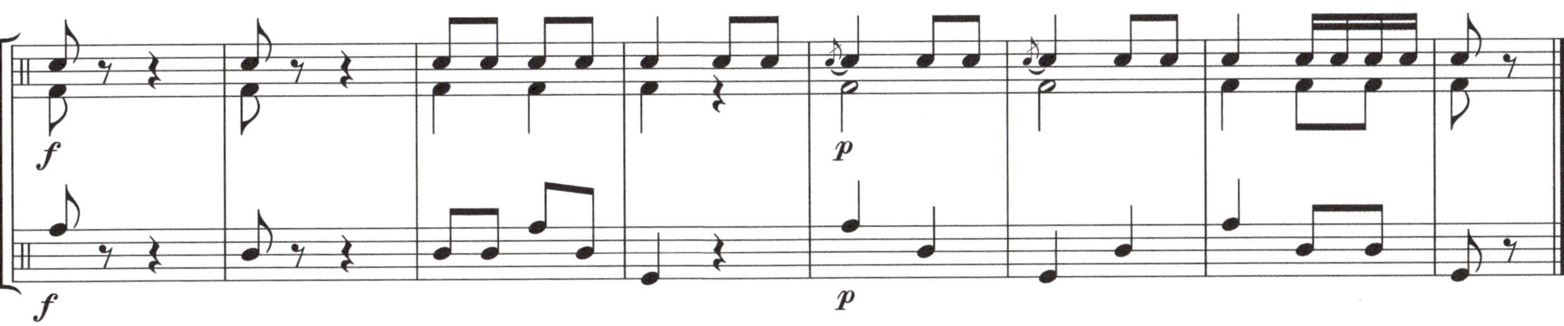

Ritardando *ritard.* (or) *rit.* - Gradually slower.

Rudiments

Flam Paradiddle

Bass Drum Roll

Similar to a timpani roll, use two bass drum mallets of equal size and roll on the same side of the drum, playing toward opposite ends of the bass drum head for best resonance.

25. GLOW WORM

Paul Lincke

Allegretto ◄ *Usually a little slower than Allegro, and with a lighter style.*

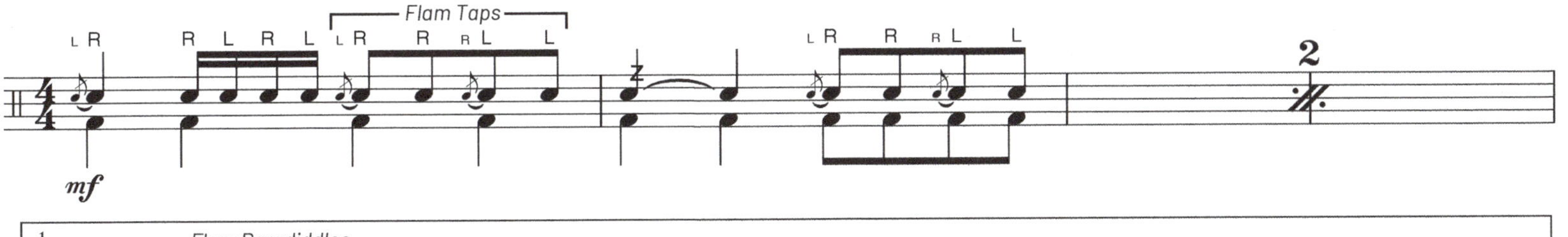

▲ *Watch your director.*

▲ *Bass Drum Roll*

26. ALMA MATER

A.C. Weekes, W.M. Smith, H.S. Thompson

26. ALMA MATER – Timpani

Tune to F and B♭

A.C. Weekes, W.M. Smith, H.S. Thompson

HISTORY

The Scottish folk song *Loch Lomond* is credited to an anonymous soldier who was imprisoned and awaiting execution. In it he writes of his desire to return home to his family and the breathtaking beauty of Loch (Lake) Lomond, a lake in Scotland. Located in the southern highlands, the lake is almost entirely surrounded by hills. One of these is Ben Lomond, a peak 3,192 feet high

Rudiment

Drag

A snare drum rudiment consisting of a double bounce and a single stroke.

27. LOCH LOMOND

Scottish Folk Song

Key Changes
(Timpani and Keyboard)

If a key signature changes during a piece of music, you will usually see a thin double bar line at the **key change**. You may also see natural signs reminding you to "cancel" previous sharps or flats. Keep playing, using the correct notes indicated in the *new* key signature.

28. MOLLY MALONE

Irish Folk Song

Dynamics

cresc. = crescendo (or)
decresc. = decrescendo (or)

29. RISE AND FALL

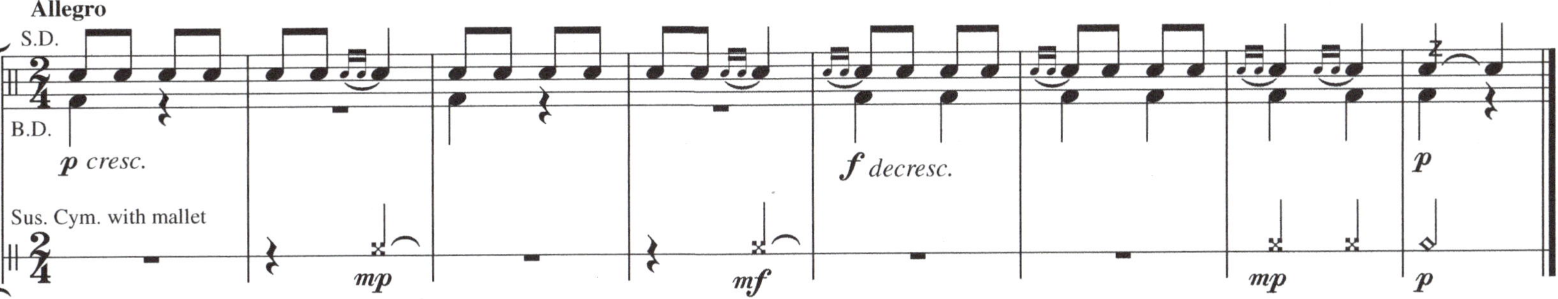

30. NO COMPARISON

31. SIGHTREADING CHALLENGE *Remember the S-T-A-R-S guidelines.*

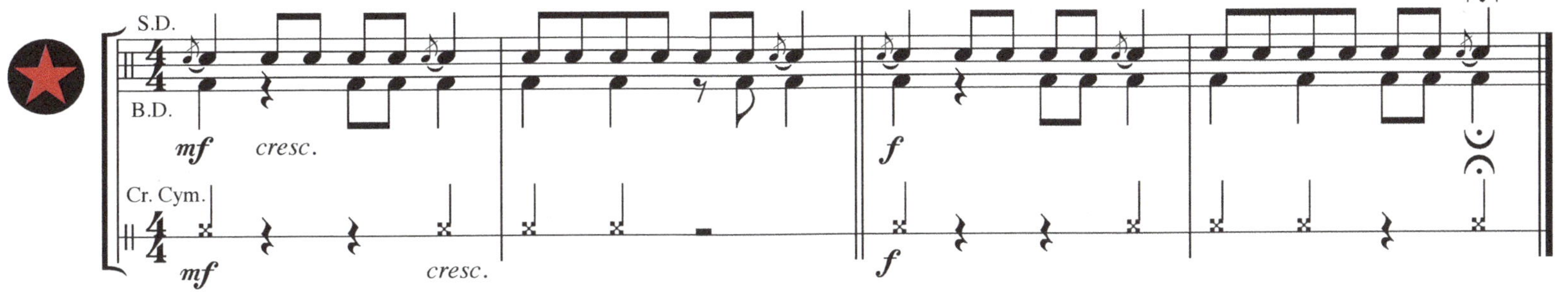

THEORY

¢ Time Signature
Cut Time (Alla Breve)

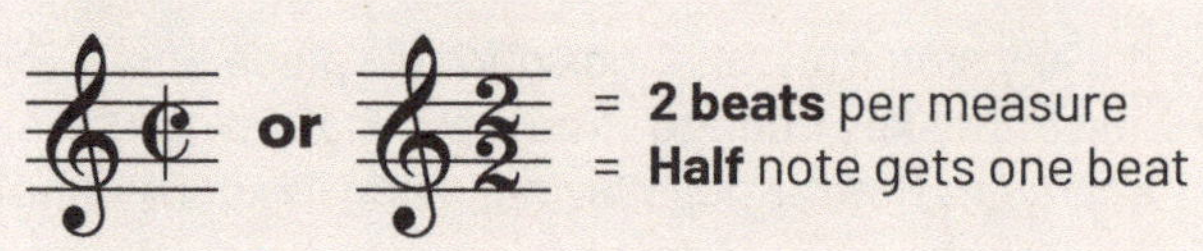

= **2 beats** per measure
= **Half** note gets one beat

𝅝 = 2 beats
𝅗𝅥 = 1 beat
♩ = ½ beat

32. RHYTHM RAP *Clap the rhythm while counting and tapping.*

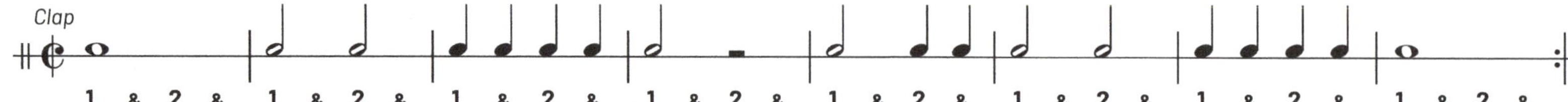

33. A CUT ABOVE

34. TWO-FOUR YANKEE DOODLE

American Folk Song

35. CUT TIME YANKEE DOODLE

American Folk Song

36. MARIANNE

Jamaican Folk Song

37. THE VICTORS *Review Right Hand Lead sticking pattern.*

Louis Elbel

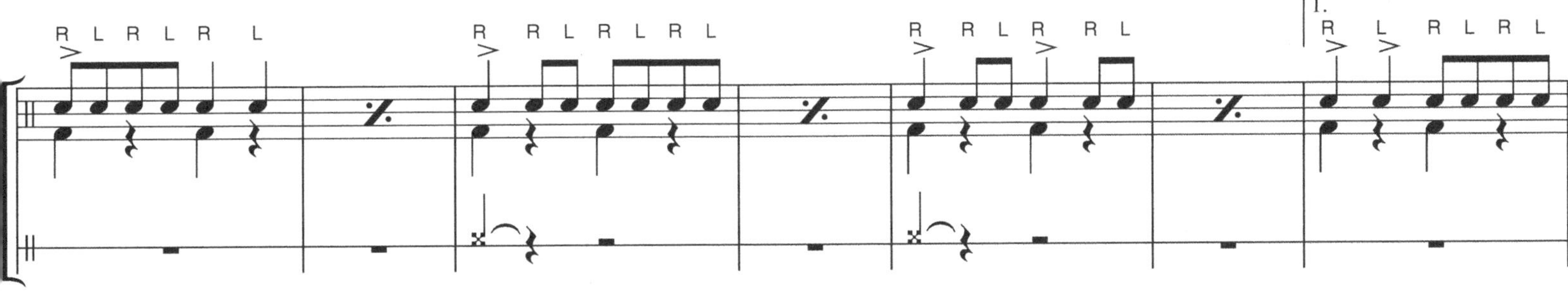

38. ESSENTIAL CREATIVITY *Write this example in cut time ₵ before playing.*

Dynamics

mp — *mezzo piano* (moderately soft)

p — *piano* (softly): brings sticks close to head
mp — *mezzo piano* (moderately soft): lift sticks a little higher
mf — *mezzo forte* (moderately loud): normal stick height
f — *forte* (loudly): lift sticks even higher

39. A - ROVING

THEORY

Syncopation

Syncopation occurs when an accent or emphasis is given to a note that is not on a strong beat. This type of "off-beat" feel is common in many popular and classical styles.

40. RHYTHM RAP

41. IN SYNC

42. LA ROCA *Optional: The Sus. Cym. and Snare Drum parts can be played by one person if desired.* Puerto Rican Folk Song

HISTORY

American composer **George M. Cohan** (1878–1942) was also a popular author, producer, director and performer. He helped develop a popular form of American musical theater now known as musical comedy. He is also considered to be one of the most famous composers of American patriotic songs, earning the Congressional Medal of Honor in 1917 for his song *Over There*. Many of his songs became morale boosters when the United States entered World War I in that same year.

43. ESSENTIAL ELEMENTS QUIZ – YOU'RE A GRAND OLD FLAG

Words and Music by George M. Cohan

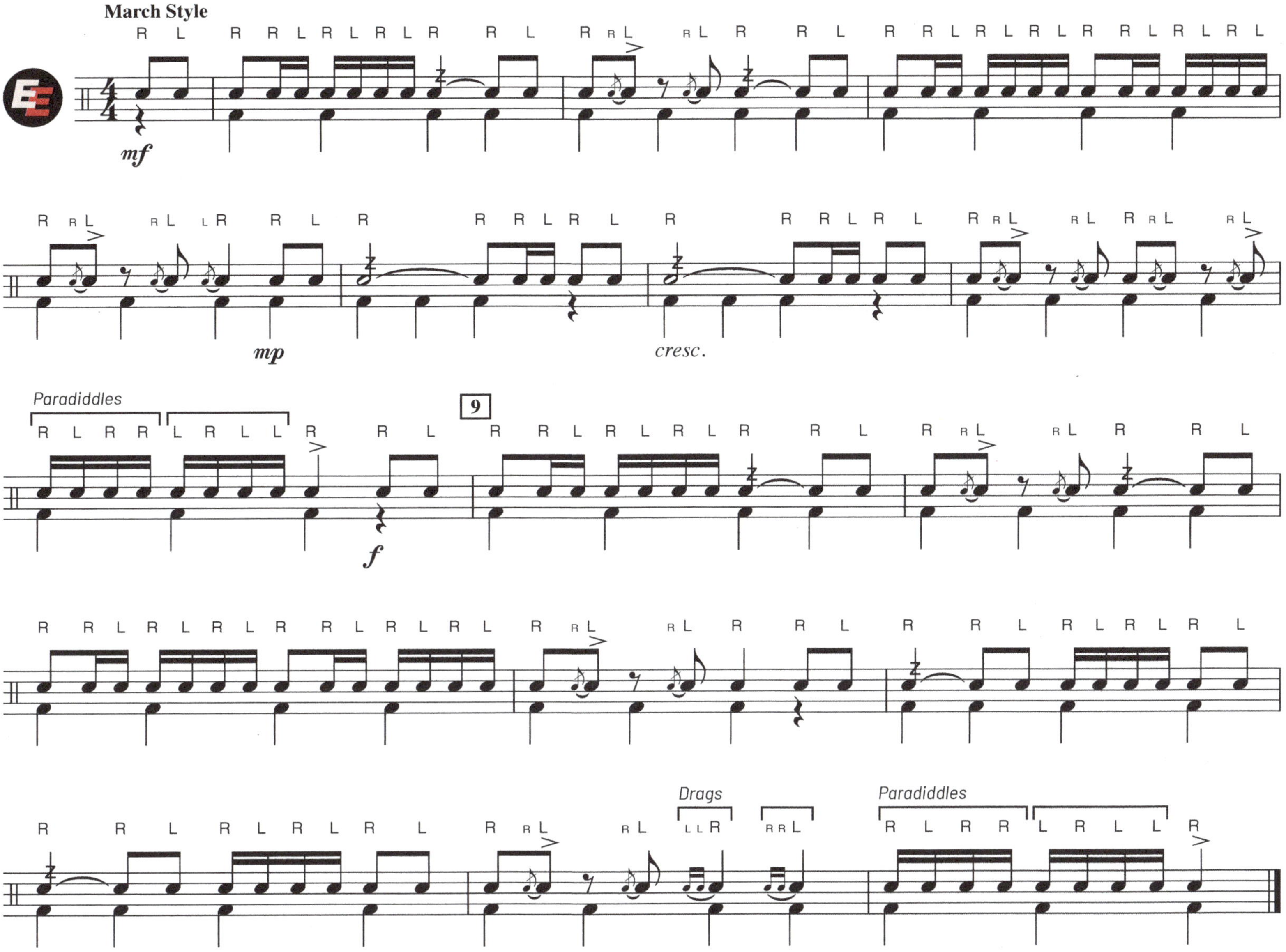
March Style
mf
mp
cresc.
Paradiddles
9
f
Drags
Paradiddles

43. ESSENTIAL ELEMENTS QUIZ – YOU'RE A GRAND OLD FLAG – Timpani

Tune to B♭ and E♭

Words and Music by George M. Cohan

March Style
mf
mp
cresc.
9
f
mp
cresc.
f

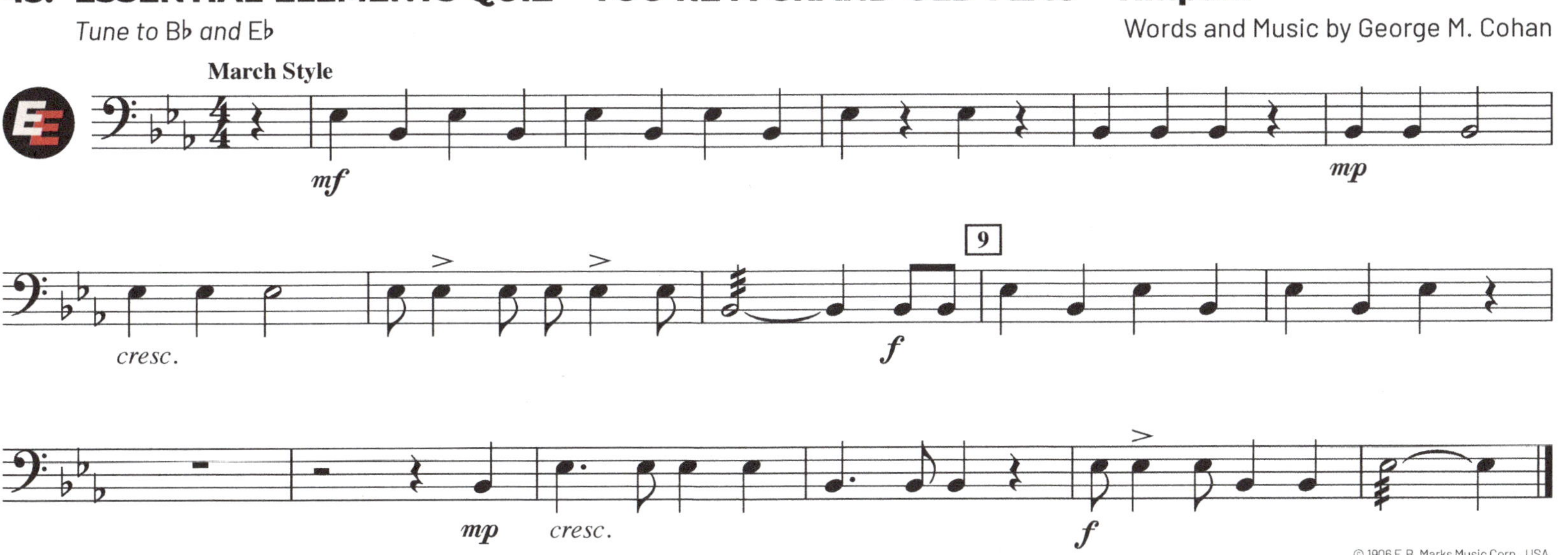

This key signature indicates your **Key of C** (no flats or sharps).

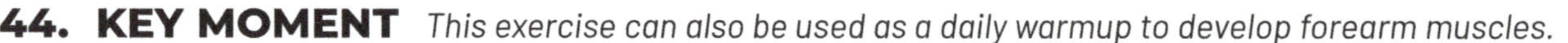

44. KEY MOMENT

This exercise can also be used as a daily warmup to develop forearm muscles.

45. THE MINSTREL BOY

Irish Folk Song

46. CLOSE CALL

47. VICTORY MARCH

M. J. Shea

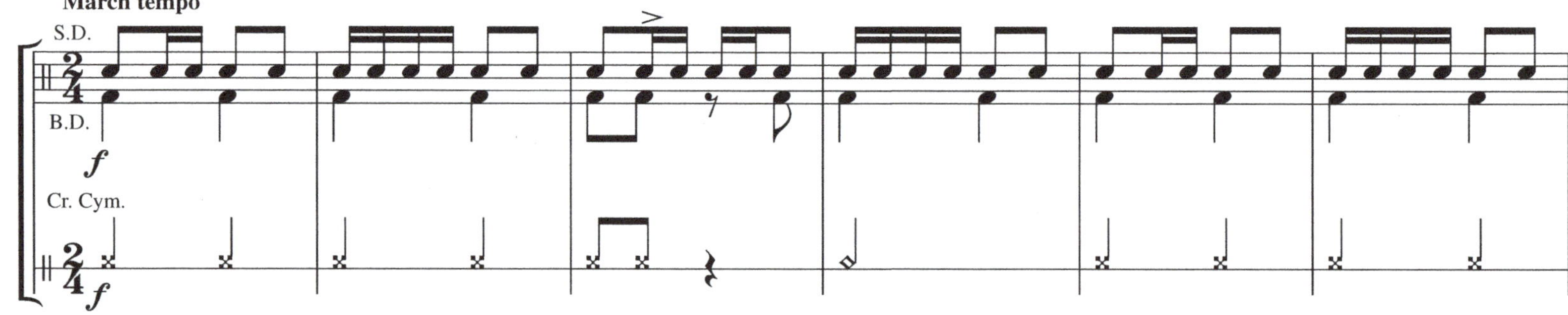

Cut Time Syncopation
(Winds and Kybd. Perc.)

2/4 ♪ ♩ ♪ = ¢ ♩ 𝅗𝅥 ♩

Compare the notation of your part below with *Victory March* on page 10-A. Should they sound the same?

THEORY

48. WINNING STREAK

M. J. Shea

49. SIGHTREADING CHALLENGE *Remember the S-T-A-R-S guidelines.*

Sixteenth Notes

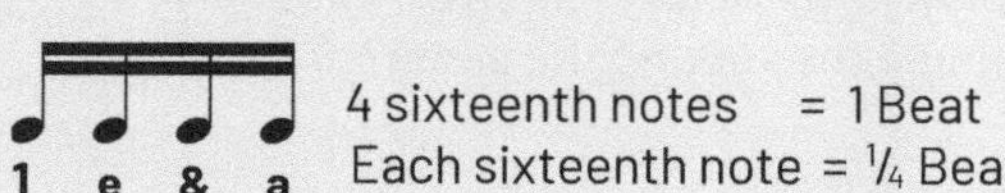

4 sixteenth notes = 1 Beat
Each sixteenth note = ¼ Beat

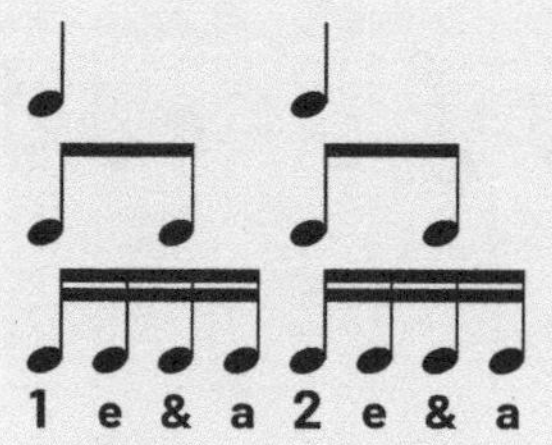

A single sixteenth note has 2 flags on the stem.

50. RHYTHM RAP

51. SIXTEENTH NOTE FANFARE

52. MOVING ALONG

Tom-Tom

Composers use this term to describe a wide variety of drums without snares. Common instruments include the double headed tom-toms on drum set, and the single headed concert tom-toms mounted on stands. Use sticks or felt mallets on the tom-tom. A snare drum with snares off may be used as a substitute.

53. BACK AND FORTH – Duet

Drum Set (Ex. 54)

The practice of one person playing several drums and cymbals in a sitting position began with the "trap drummers" in the late 1890's and early 1900's in travelling shows, the circus, and the theatre pit. Today, drum set has become an important part of many styles of music groups including jazz ensembles, rock 'n' roll bands, and pit orchestras.

To learn the basics, start with the three primary sounds of a drum set:

Suspended Cymbal – usually called the "Ride Cymbal" and played with the right hand.

Snare Drum – played with the left hand.

Bass Drum – played with a foot pedal.

Drum Set notation

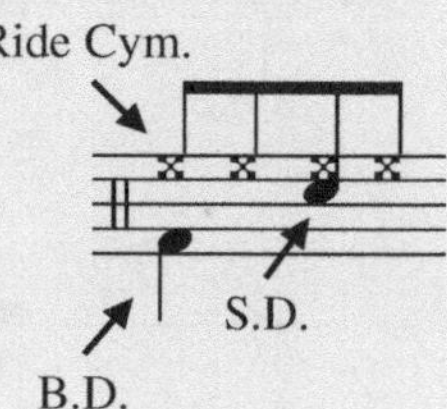

54. COMIN' ROUND THE MOUNTAIN VARIATIONS

American Folk Song

54. COMIN' ROUND THE MOUNTAIN VARIATIONS – Timpani

American Folk Song

Tune to F and C

55. ESSENTIAL ELEMENTS QUIZ

Use Flam Paradiddle Sticking when playing the 16th note groups.

PERFORMANCE SPOTLIGHT

56. WARM-UP CHORALE

J. S. Bach/Arr. by John Higgins

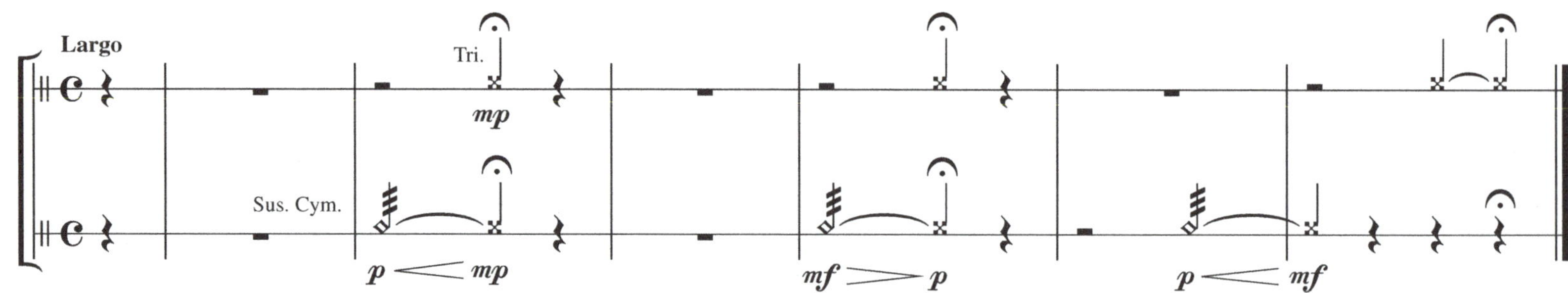

57. THE THUNDERER – Band Arrangement

Snare Drum, Bass Drum

John Philip Sousa
Arr. by John Higgins

57. THE THUNDERER – Band Arrangement

Crash Cymbal

John Philip Sousa
Arr. by John Higgins

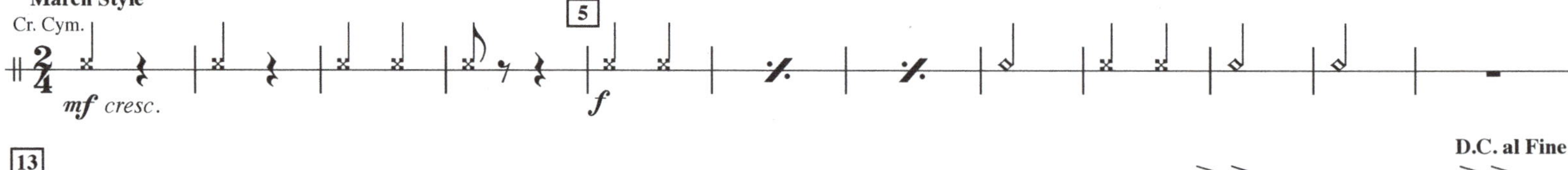

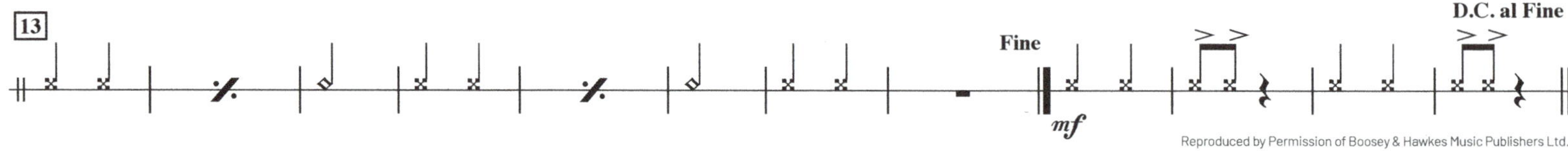

Bongos
(Ex. 58)

Bongos are the highest pitched hand drums in the Latin American percussion family. Traditionally, bongos with skin heads are played with the fingers while sitting down, holding the bongos between the knees with the larger drum on the right. Bongos are also available with plastic heads mounted on a stand. These bongos can be played with thin sticks or small, hard felt mallets.

58. HILL AND GULLY RIDER – Band Arrangement

Bongos, Bass Drum

Jamaican Folk Song
Arr. by John Higgins

58. HILL AND GULLY RIDER – Band Arrangement

Maracas, Claves

Jamaican Folk Song
Arr. by John Higgins

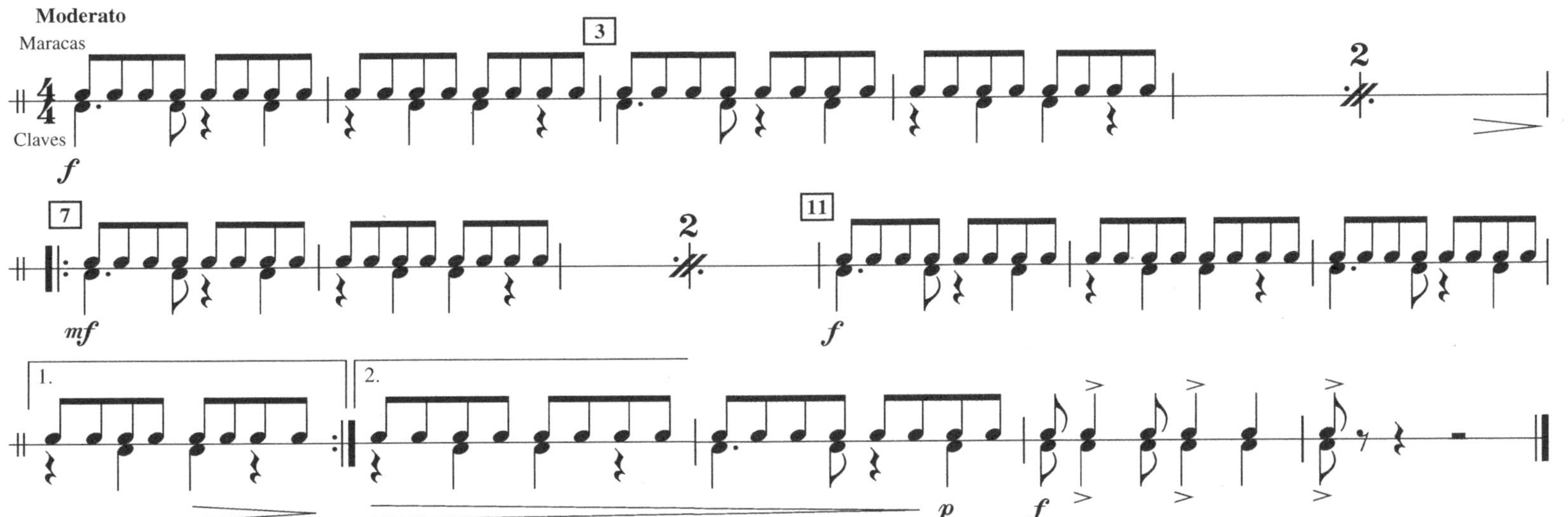

59. SHENANDOAH – Band Arrangement

Snare Drum, Bass Drum

American Folk Song
Arr. by John Higgins

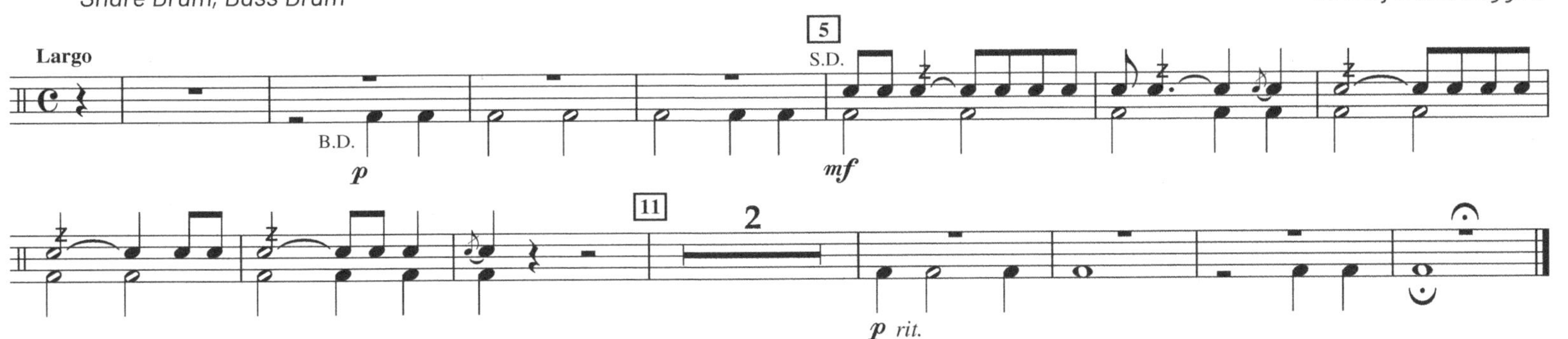

59. SHENANDOAH – Band Arrangement

Suspended Cymbal

American Folk Song
Arr. by John Higgins

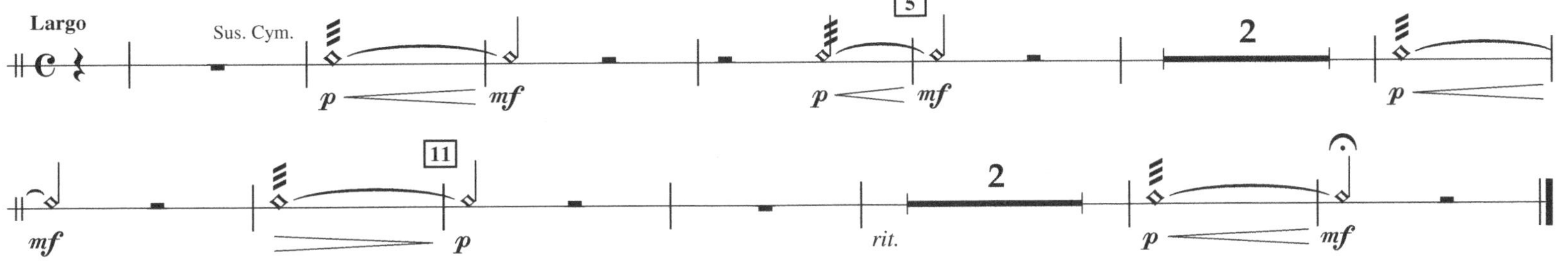

PERFORMANCE SPOTLIGHT

Guiro

The guiro (pronounced *we' ro*) is a Latin American instrument usually in the shape of a gourd with hollowed-out notches on the side. It is played by scraping a stick along the notched side. A good sound will result if you keep constant pressure on the stick while scraping.

Cross Stick Rim Shot

Place the tip of the left stick in the middle of the head and gently strike the left stick with the right just in front of where you are holding the stick.

60. LAS MAÑANITAS – Band Arrangement

Snare Drum, Bass Drum

Mexican Folk Song
Arr. by John Higgins

Allegro
Snares off
S.D.
B.D.
f *mf* 3
Cross Stick Rim Shots 11 *f*
Cross Stick Rim Shots 19 C.S.R.S. *p* *cresc.*
f C.S.R.S. 1. 2.

60. LAS MAÑANITAS – Band Arrangement

Guiro, Claves

Mexican Folk Song
Arr. by John Higgins

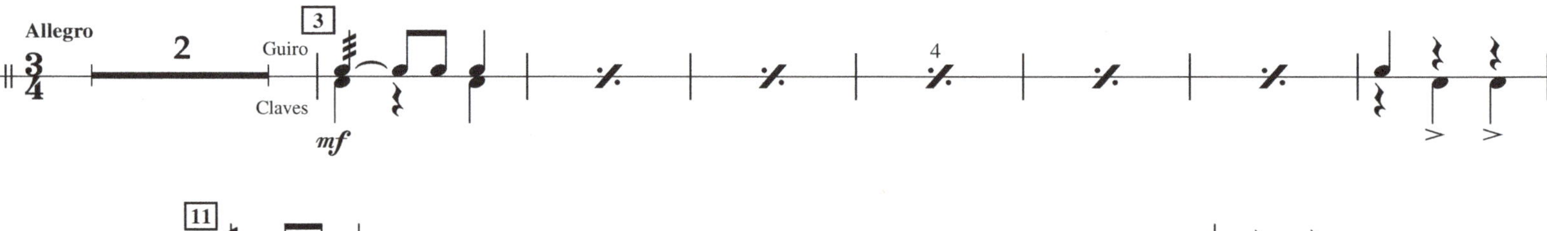

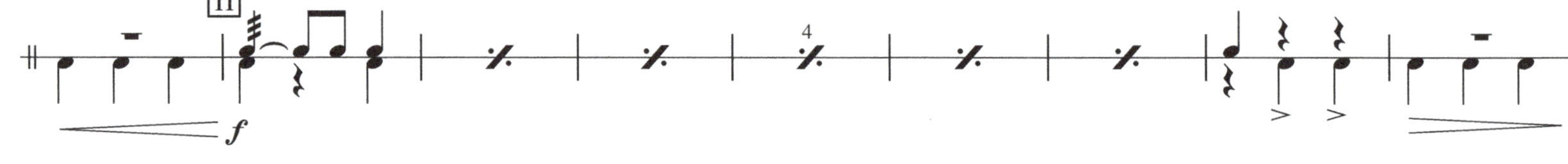

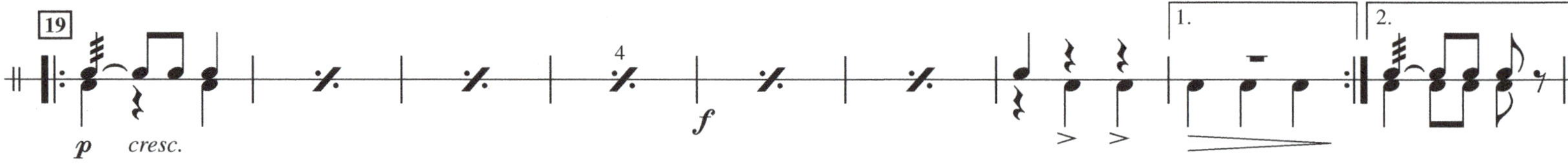

61. RONDEAU – Band Arrangement
Snare Drum, Bass Drum
Jean-Joseph Mouret
Arr. by John Higgins
March Style
f
1.
2.
D.S. al Fine–Go back to the sign (𝄋) and play until Fine.
Fine
D.S. al Fine
61. RONDEAU – Band Arrangement – Timpani
Tune to B♭ and E♭
Jean-Joseph Mouret
Arr. by John Higgins
March Style
f
1.
D.S. al Fine–Go back to the sign (𝄋) and play until Fine.
2.
Fine
D.S. al Fine
62. ROCK.COM – Encore Band Arrangement
Snare Drum, Bass Drum
John Higgins
Moderato
Opt. Drum Set
Ride Cym.
S.D.
B.D.
f
2
9
mp
f
f
1.
2.
62. ROCK.COM – Encore Band Arrangement
Cowbell
John Higgins
Moderato
Cowbell
f
4
9
4
f
1.
2.

63. RHYTHM RAP

64. SIXTEENTH VARIATIONS

Tambourine Knee to Fist Technique

The preferred method for playing rapid passages is the knee to fist technique. Position your foot on a small stool so that the knee is raised. Hold the tambourine above your knee with the head facing down and close your other hand over the open end of the tambourine to form a fist. Move the tambourine to the knee (it should bounce off of the top of the knee), then up to the closed fist, following the K and F markings in the music.

65. SEA CHANTEY

66. AMERICAN FANFARE

New Key Signature
(Keyboard Percussion)

This key signature indicates your **Key of A♭**. Play all B's as B-flat, all E's as E-flat, all A's as A-flat, and all D's as D-flat.

THEORY

Flam Rudiment Review

This exercise includes Flam Taps (measures 1-2), Flam Paradiddles (measures 3-4), and Flams (measures 4 and 7). Observe all stickings carefully.

67. SCALE STUDY

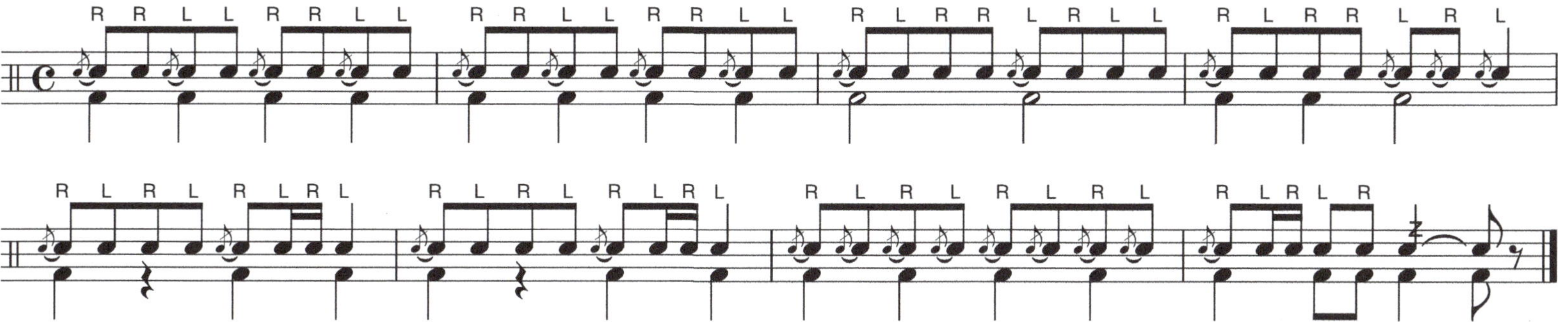

Crash Cymbal Chokes
(Hi-Hat Style)

Hold the cymbals in a horizontal position with the edges of the cymbals closed against your stomach and open facing away from you. Using the edges close to your stomach as a hinge, close the cymbals on the beats, and open them on the rests.

68. BILL BAILEY

Hughie Cannon

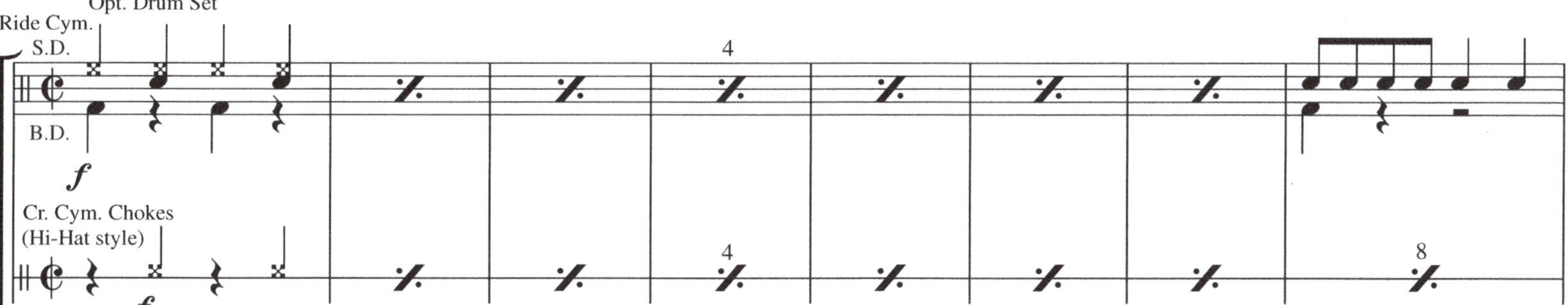

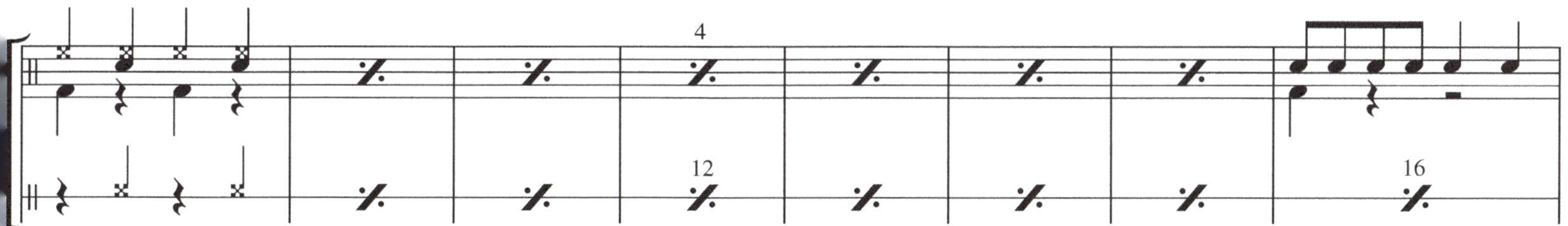

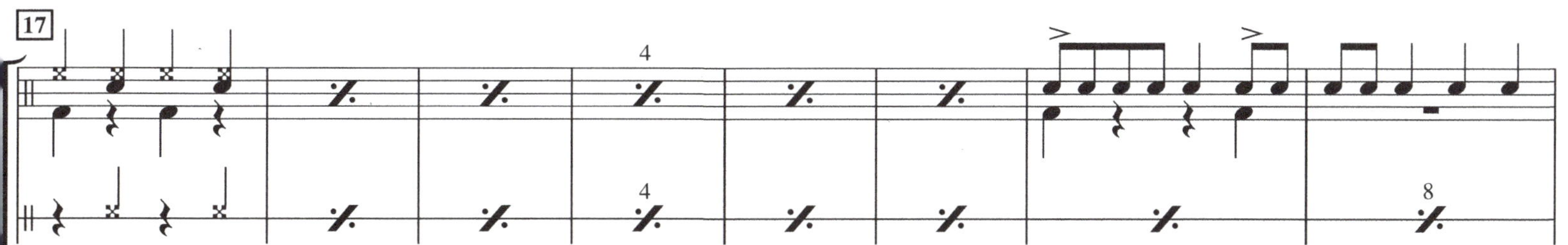

69. RHYTHM RAP

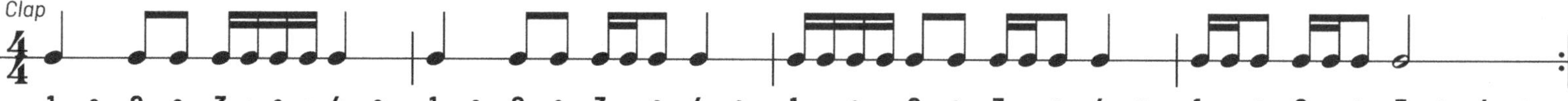

70. RHYTHM ETUDE

71. BATTLE STATIONS

72. ENGLISH DANCE

Tambourine Sixteenth Note Technique

Hold the tambourine in a vertical position. To play four sixteenth notes, move the tambourine toward the opposite hand, then back, then move the tambourine to the heel of the opposite hand (for the accent), then back. Repeat for each group of sixteenth notes.

73. BIG ROCK CANDY MOUNTAIN

American Folk Song

74. ESSENTIAL ELEMENTS QUIZ

Rallentando

rall. - Gradually slower (same as *ritardando*).

75. SIMPLE SONG – Duet

76. LINE DANCE *Review the Flamacue Rudiment.*

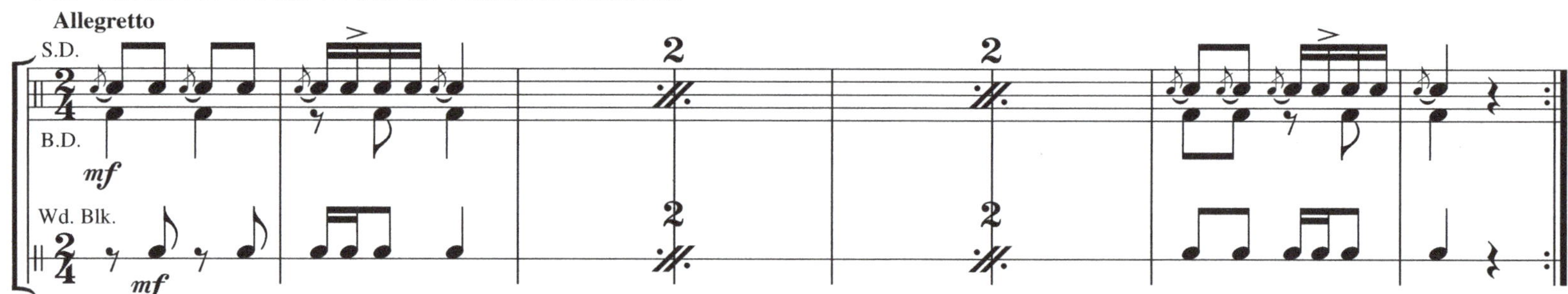

77. TECHNIQUE TRAX

78. THE GALWAY PIPER

Irish Reel

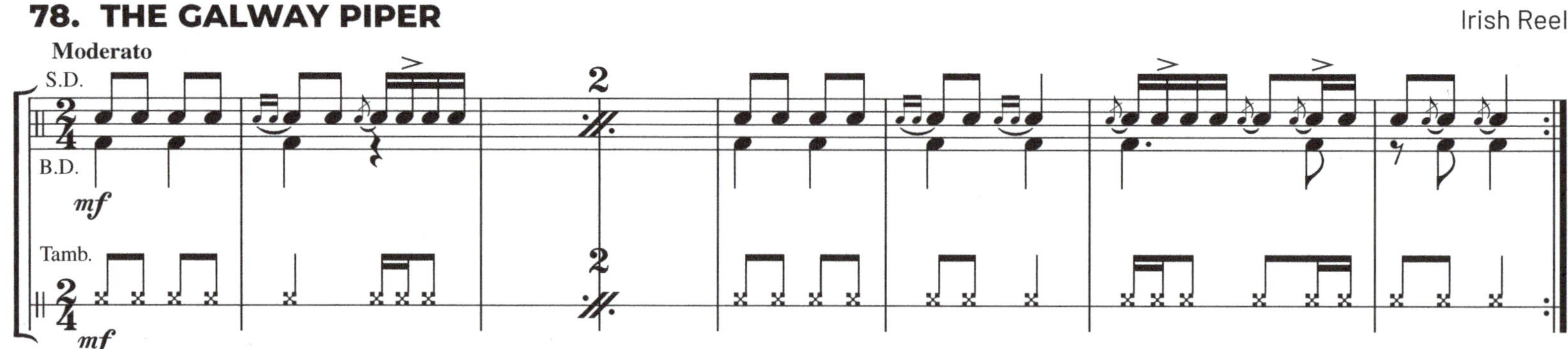

79. MANHATTAN BEACH MARCH

John Philip Sousa

80. SIGHTREADING CHALLENGE *Remember the S-T-A-R-S guidelines.*

81. RHYTHM RAP

82. MARCHING ALONG

83. FANFARE FOR BAND – Trio

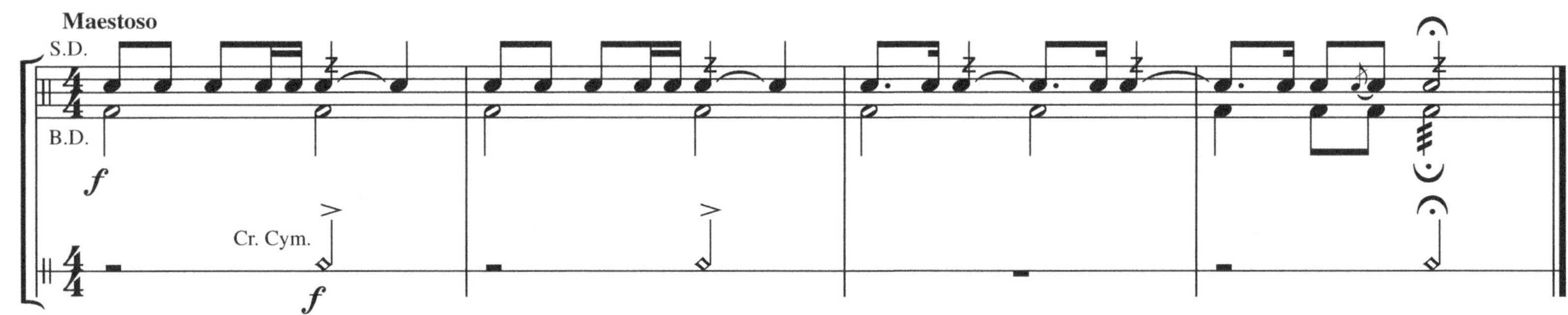

84. O TANNENBAUM

German Carol

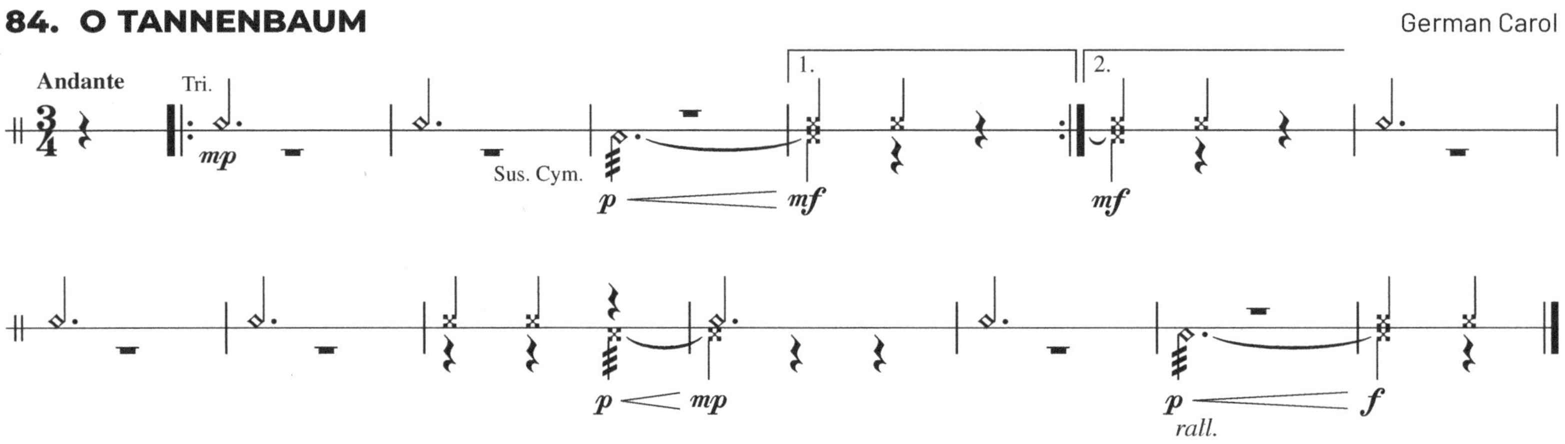

84. O TANNENBAUM – Timpani

German Carol

Tune to B♭ and E♭

85. S'VIVON

Traditional Hanukkah Song

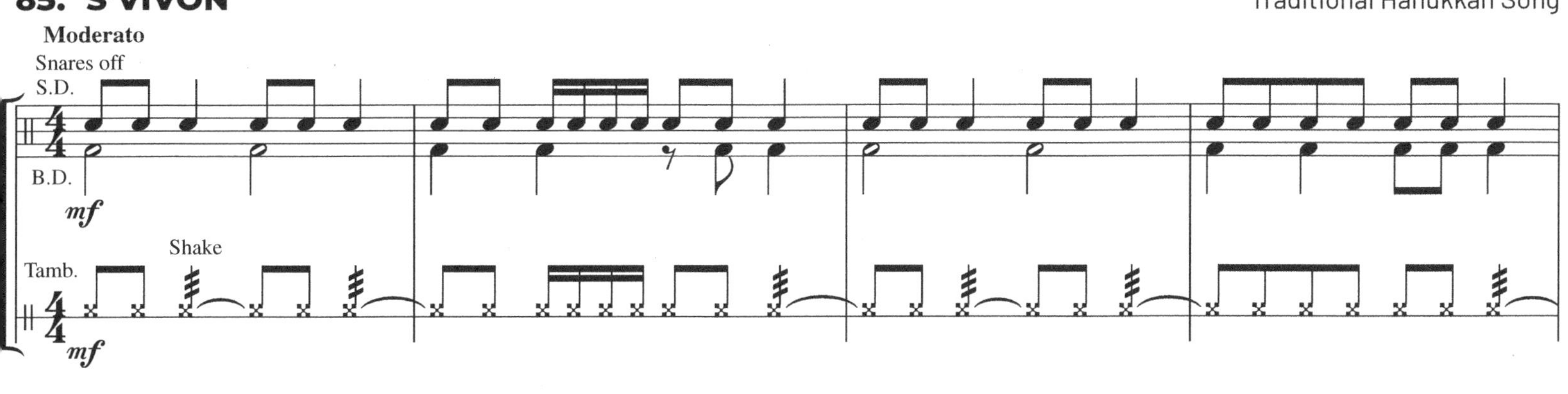

86. GOOD KING WENCESLAS

English Carol

DAILY WARM-UPS

WORK-OUTS FOR TONE & TECHNIQUE

Double Bounce

A double bounce is a controlled multiple bounce consisting of only two bounces per stroke. Rolls that use double bounces are called **open** (measured) rolls.

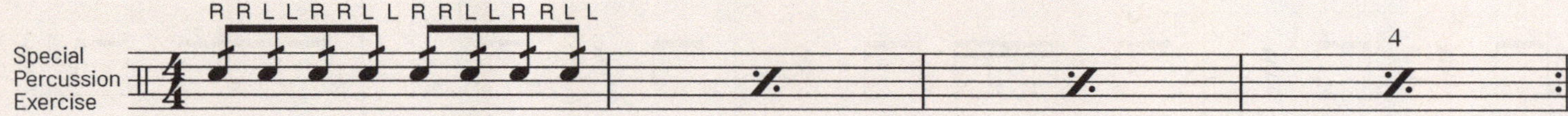

87. TONE BUILDER *Play at a very slow tempo.*

This exercise shows the correct number of hand motions and strokes for the ***Five Stroke Roll*** *(measures 2–4) and the* ***Nine Stroke Roll*** *(measure 5). Use the Double Bounce Technique of one hand motion for two strokes (bounces).*

88. FLEXIBILITY STUDY

This example shows how open five stroke rolls are written in music.
Use the same technique from the previous exercise for these rolls.

89. TECHNIQUE TRAX

This example shows how open nine stroke rolls are written in music. Use the same technique from Ex. 87 for these rolls.

90. CHORALE

Johann Sebastian Bach

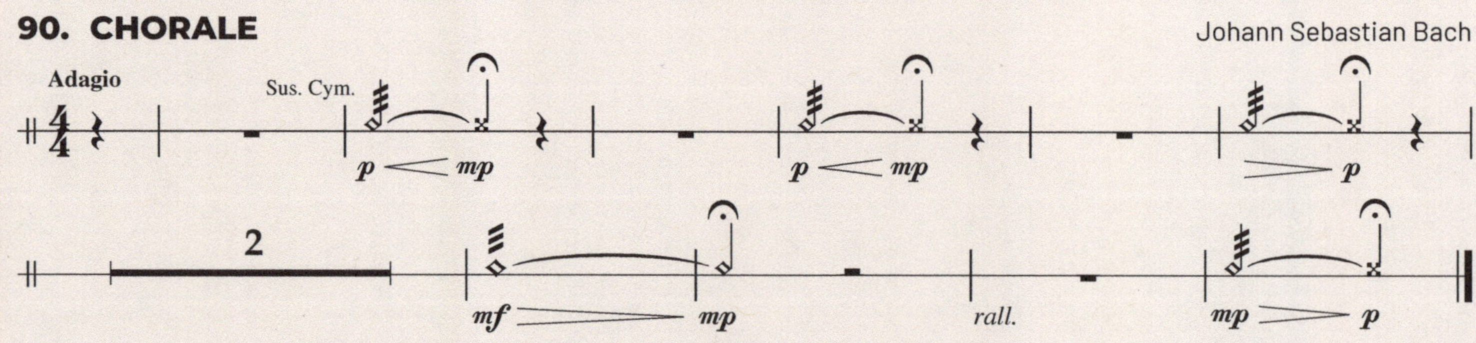

90. CHORALE – Timpani

Johann Sebastian Bach

Tune to F and B♭

Adagio
p
mp
p
mf
mp
rall.
p

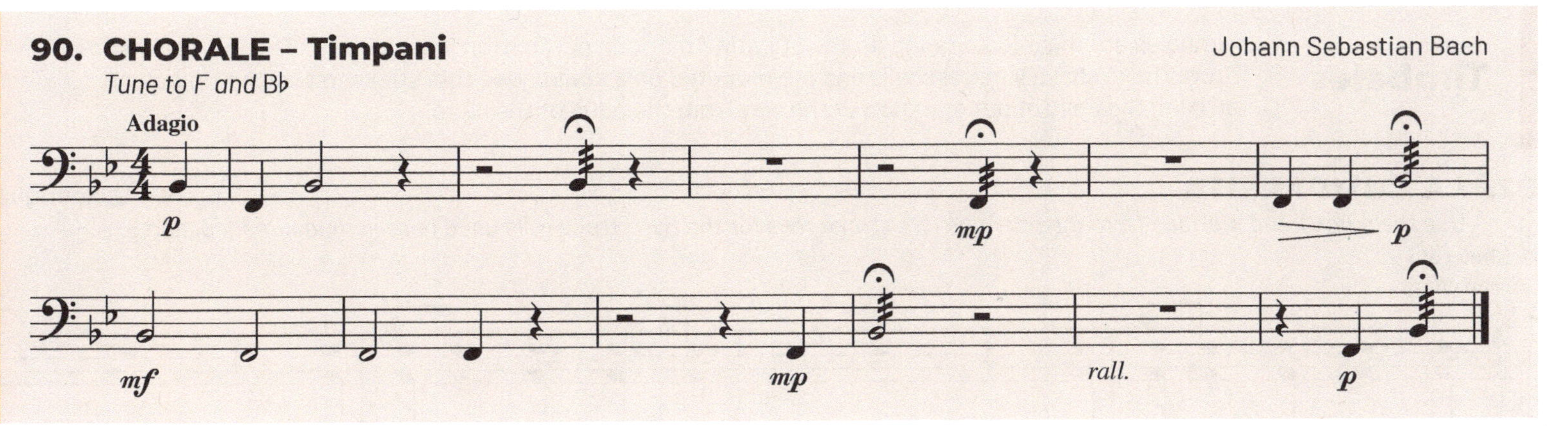

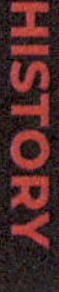

French composer **Georges Bizet** (1838–1875) entered the Paris Conservatory to study music when he was only ten years old. There he won many awards for voice, piano, organ, and composition. Bizet's best known composition is the opera *Carmen*, which was first performed in 1875. *Carmen* tells the story of a band of Gypsies, soldiers, smugglers, and outlaws. Originally criticized for its realism on stage, it was soon hailed as the most popular French opera ever written.

HISTORY

91. TOREADOR SONG (from CARMEN)

Georges Bizet

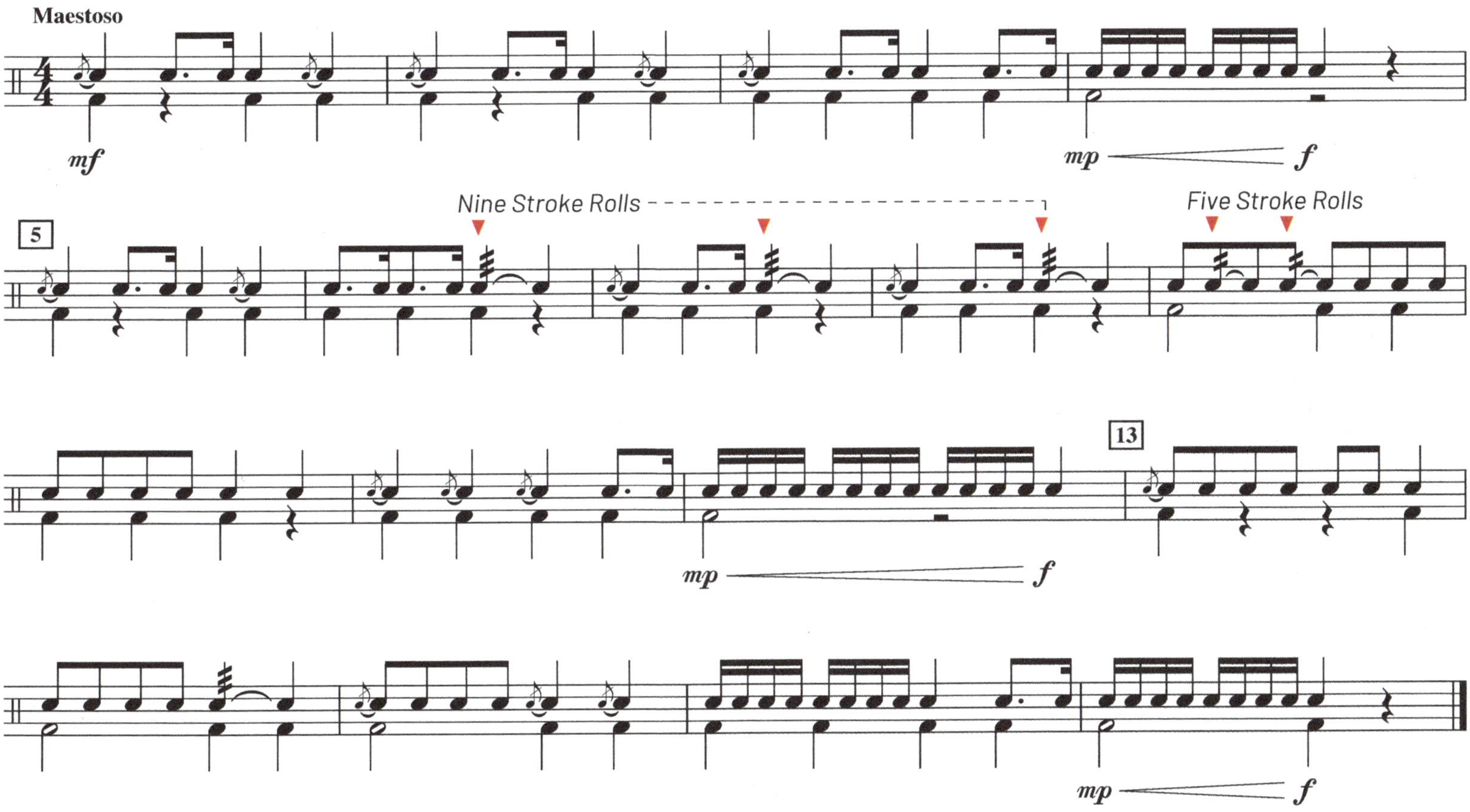

Maestoso
mf
mp
f
5
Nine Stroke Rolls
Five Stroke Rolls
13
mp
f
mp
f

91. TOREADOR SONG (from CARMEN) – Timpani

Georges Bizet

Tune to B♭ and E♭

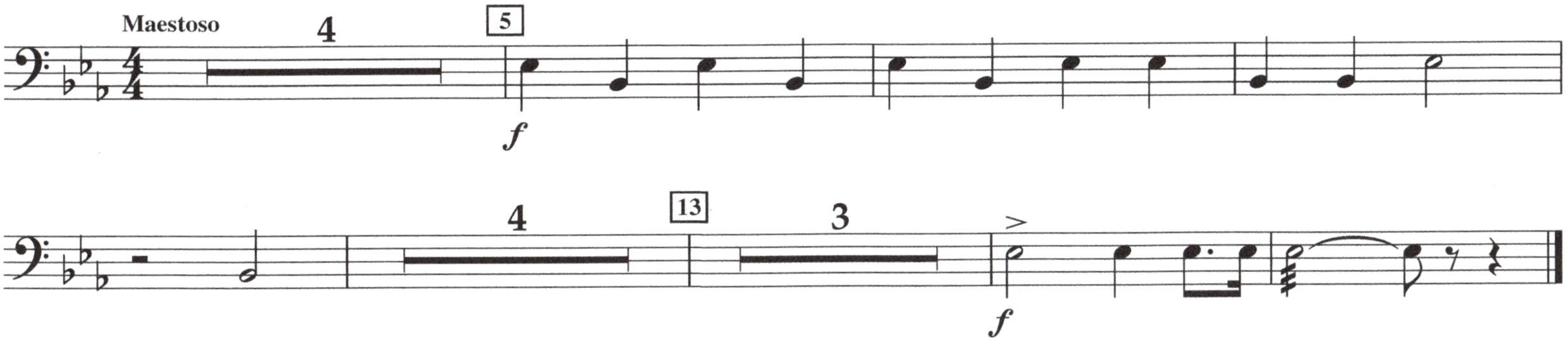

Maestoso
4
5
f
4
13
3
f

Timbales

Timbales are the middle range drums of Latin American percussion instruments. These single headed drums have shallow metal shells and are mounted on a stand. Use thin sticks to play the timbales, striking the head about one third of the way from the edge of the head.

92. LA CUMPARSITA

G. Rodriguez

Use the same hand motions from the previous five stroke rolls for the five stroke rolls used here in measures 1, 3, and 5.

Moderato

Snares off

S.D.

B.D.

mf

Timbales

mf

Stick Clicks

93. THE YELLOW ROSE OF TEXAS

American Folk Song

Moderato

S.D.

B.D.

mf

Cr. Cym.

mf

94. SCALE STUDY

Use the same hand motions from the previous nine stroke rolls for the nine stroke rolls used here in measures 1, 3, 4, and 8.

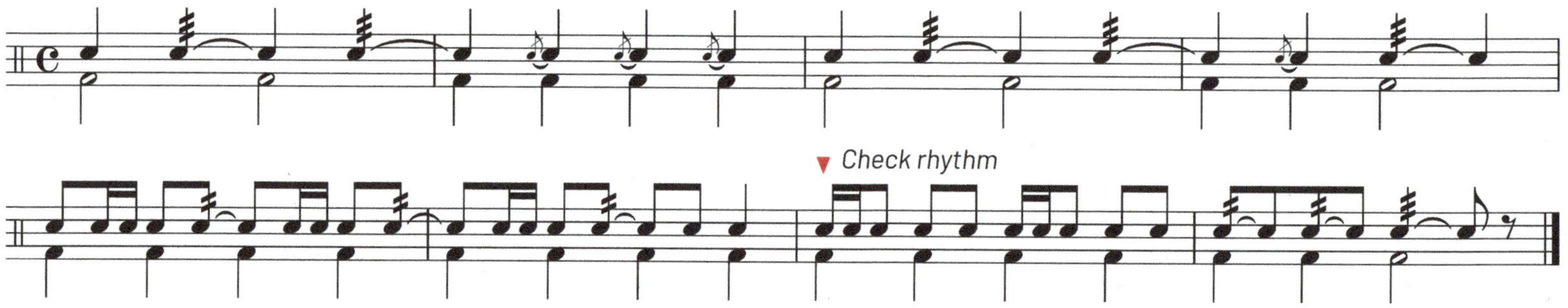

HISTORY

Until 1974 Australia's official national anthem was *God Save The Queen*. A competition was held in 1973 to compose a new anthem, but none of the entries met with the judges' approval. Finally the government asked the public to vote, choosing from among Australia's 3 most popular patriotic songs. After easily defeating *Waltzing Matilda* and *God Save The Queen*, *Advance Australia Fair* was officially declared the national anthem of Australia on April 19, 1974.

95. ADVANCE AUSTRALIA FAIR

Peter Dodds McCormick

Maestoso

f *mp* *f* *mp*

9

cresc. *f*

rit. *a tempo*

▲ Resume previous tempo

96. ESSENTIAL CREATIVITY

Arrange the melody of "America (My Country 'Tis Of Thee)" for keyboard percussion. Write out the first line (6 measures). Your first note is F. ADD: Key signature—key of F • Time signature—3/4 • Tempo and dynamic markings.

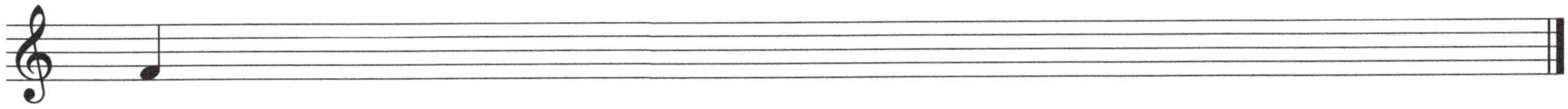

Play the completed line on keyboard percussion to hear your own version.

97. AMERICAN PATROL

F. W. Meacham

98. ARIA (from MARRIAGE OF FIGARO)

Wolfgang Amadeus Mozart

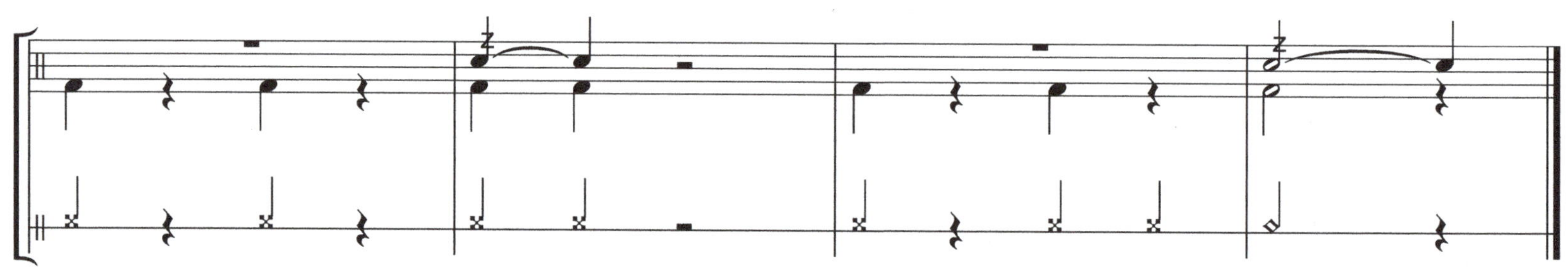

HISTORY

(Ex. 99)
American composer **John Philip Sousa** (1854–1932) was best known for his brilliant band marches. Sousa wrote 136 marches, including *The Stars and Stripes Forever*, which was declared the official march of the United States of America in 1987.

99. THE STARS AND STRIPES FOREVER

John Philip Sousa

March Tempo

S.D.
B.D.
Cr. Cym.

f

17

mp *f*

mp *f*

100. SIGHTREADING CHALLENGE *Remember the S-T-A-R-S guidelines.*

THEORY

6/8 Time Signature

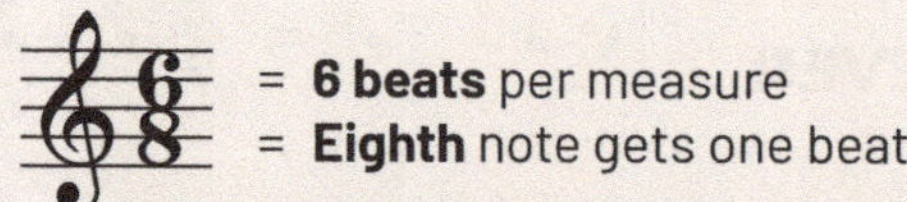

♪ = 1 beat ♩ = 2 beats
♩. = 3 beats 𝅗𝅥. = 6 beats

6/8 time is usually played with a slight emphasis on the **1st** and **4th** beats of each measure. This divides the measure into 2 groups of 3 beats each. In faster music, these two primary beats will make the music feel like it's counted "in 2."

101. RHYTHM RAP *Clap the rhythm while counting and tapping.*

102. LAZY DAY

Multiple Bounce in 6/8 Time Signature

Use the sticking pattern from the eighth note pulse and connect with multiple bounces to sound as smooth as possible.

103. ROW YOUR BOAT

104. JOLLY GOOD FELLOW

105. CHANSON

French Folk Song

106. ESSENTIAL ELEMENTS QUIZ – WHEN JOHNNY COMES MARCHING HOME

American Folk Song

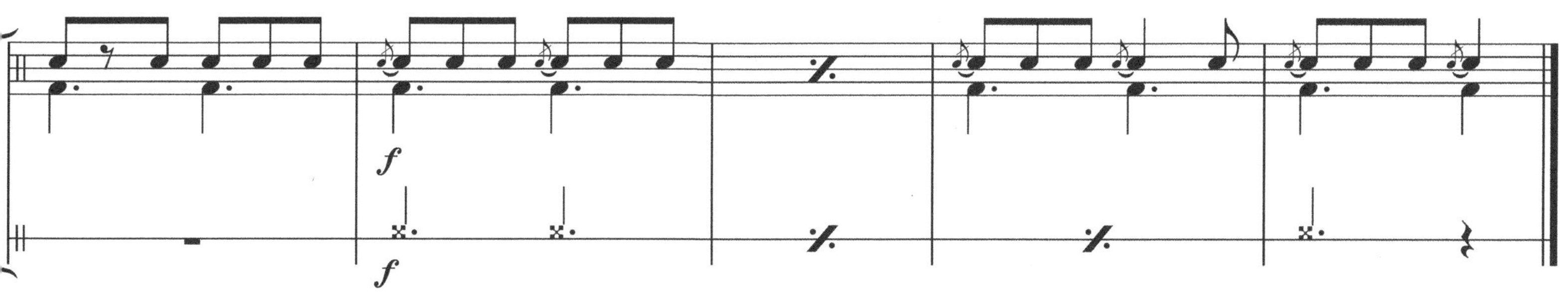

THEORY

More Enharmonics

Remember that notes which sound the same but have different letter names are called **enharmonics**. These are some common enharmonics that are used in keybd. perc. in the exercises below.

More Chromatics

The smallest distance between two notes is a half-step, and a scale made up of consecutive half-steps is a **chromatic scale**. These are usually written with **enharmonic** notes—sharps when going up and flats when going down.

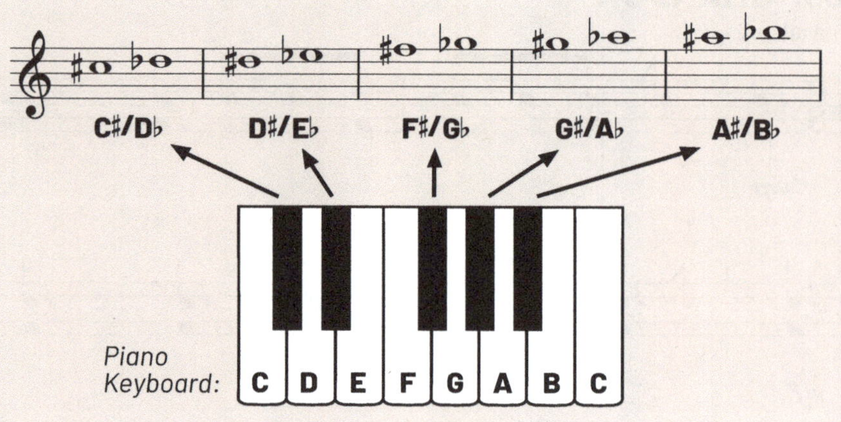

107. CHROMATIC SCALE

Note: The sixteenth notes preceding the 17 stroke rolls use the same number of hand motions. The hand motions never change speed; just go from single strokes to double bounces (open rolls).

108. TECHNIQUE TRAX

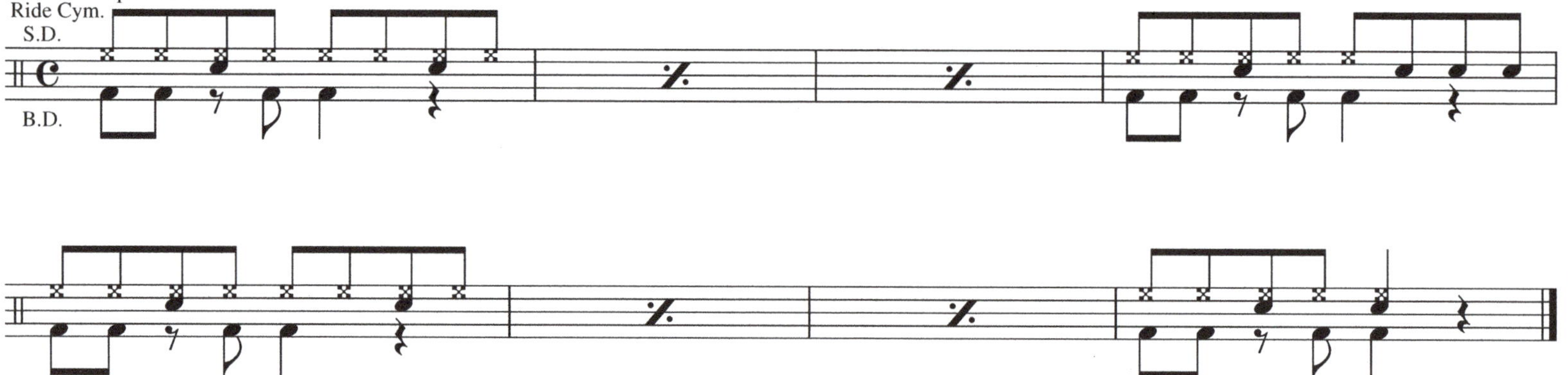

A **Habañera** is a Cuban dance and song form in slow 2/4 meter. It is named after the city of Havana, the capital of Cuba. Made popular in the New World in the early 19th Century, it was later carried over to Spain. There the rhythms of the Habañera were incorporated into many styles of Latin music. One of the most famous Habañeras is heard in Bizet's *Carmen*, written in 1875.

HISTORY

Tambourine Thumb Roll

In addition to the tambourine shake, another method of producing a sustained sound on the tambourine is the thumb roll. Holding the tambourine in the left hand, begin by placing the right thumb at 3 o'clock on the head. Move the thumb slowly with slight pressure in a counter-clockwise direction toward 9 o'clock. The proper combination of thumb pressure and slow speed will produce a sustained sound on the tambourine.

109. HABAÑERA (from CARMEN)

Georges Bizet

110. CHROMATIC CRESCENDO

111. TURKISH MARCH (from THE RUINS OF ATHENS)

Ludwig van Beethoven

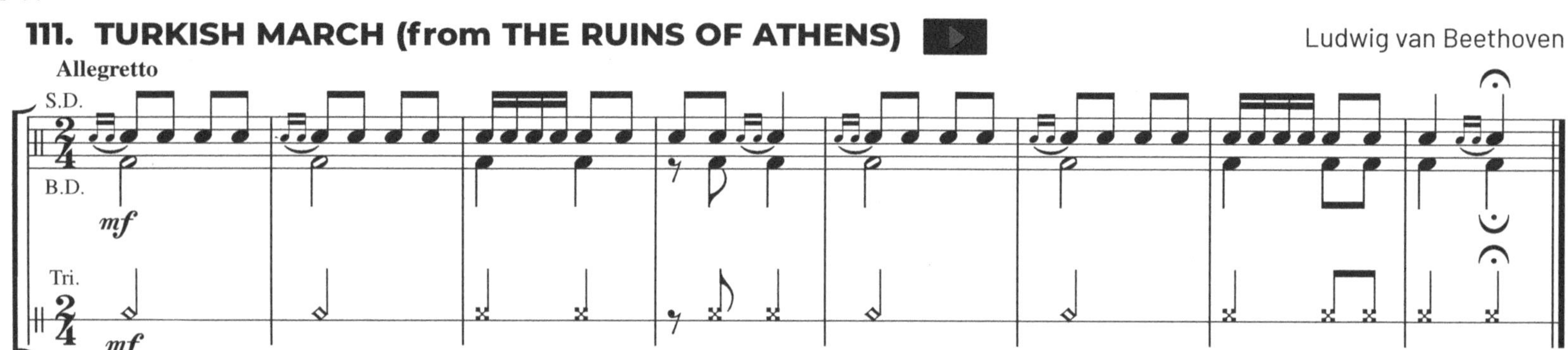

112. THE OVERLANDER

Australian Folk Song

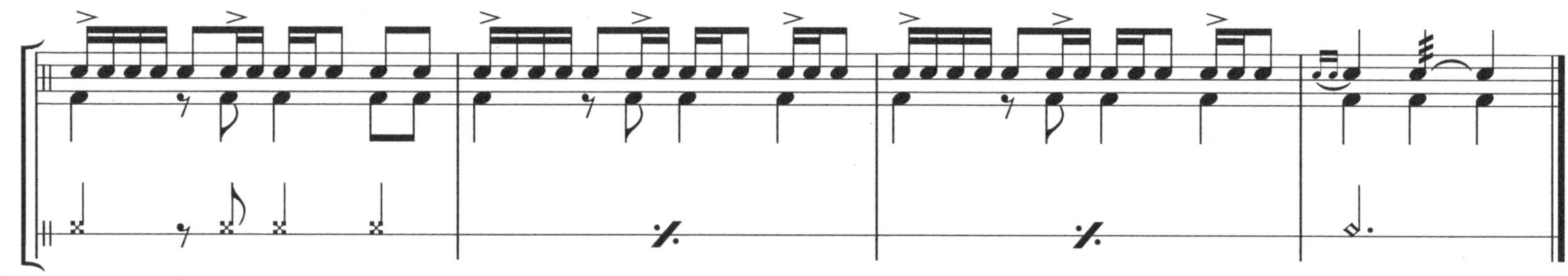

113. STACCATO STUDY

Review the double sticking patterns used in this example. Can you identify the rudiment in measure 4?

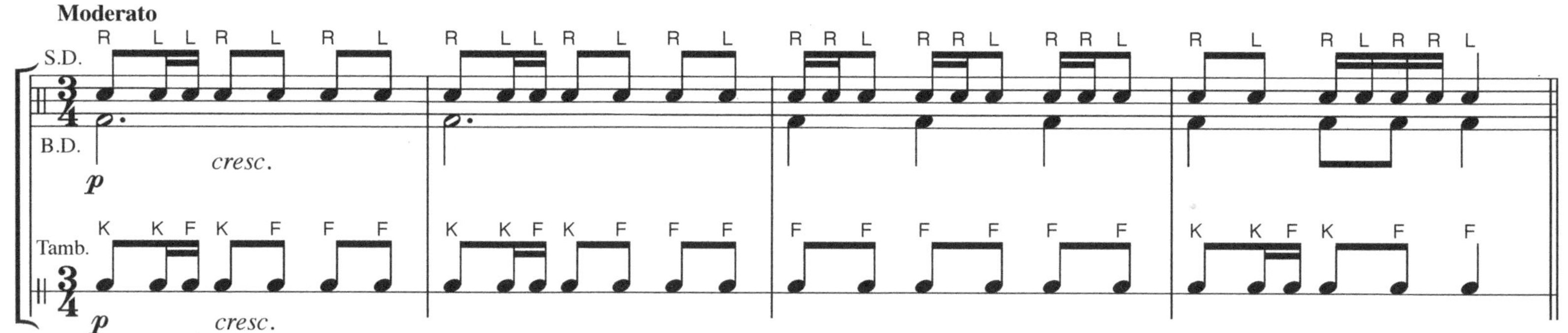

Tambourine players should review the knee to fist technique on page 14-A.

Listen for the key change. ▲

114. YANKEE DOODLE DANDY

Words and Music by George M. Cohan

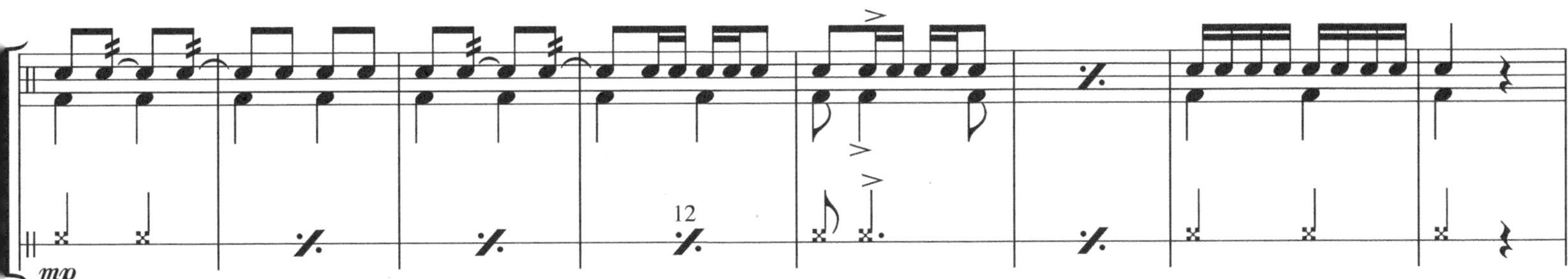

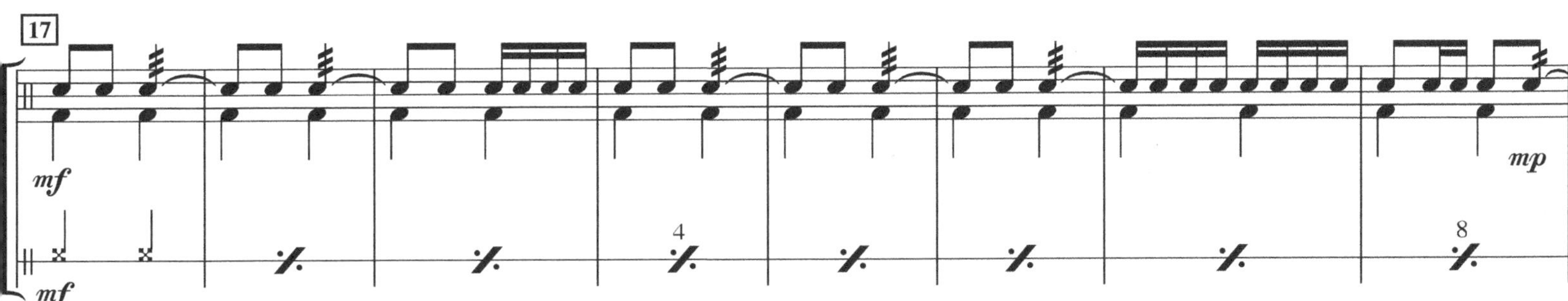

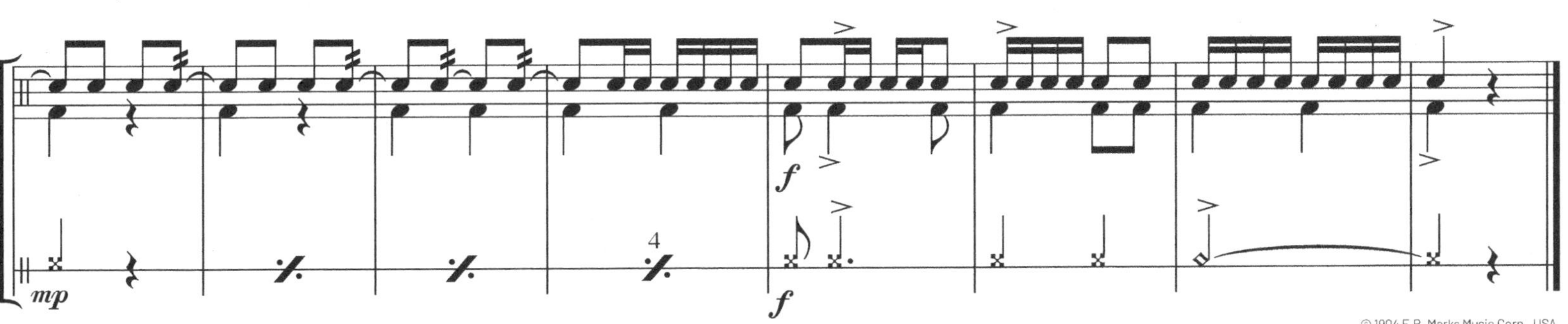

115. SIGHTREADING CHALLENGE

Remember the **S-T-A-R-S** guidelines:
S – Sharps or flats in the key signature, **T** – Time signature and tempos, **A** – Accidentals, **R** – Rhythm, **S** – Signs

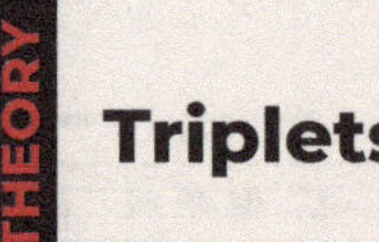

Triplets

A **triplet** is a group of **3** notes played in the space of **2**. In $\frac{2}{4}$, $\frac{3}{4}$, or $\frac{4}{4}$ time, an eighth note triplet is spread evenly across one beat.

116. RHYTHM RAP

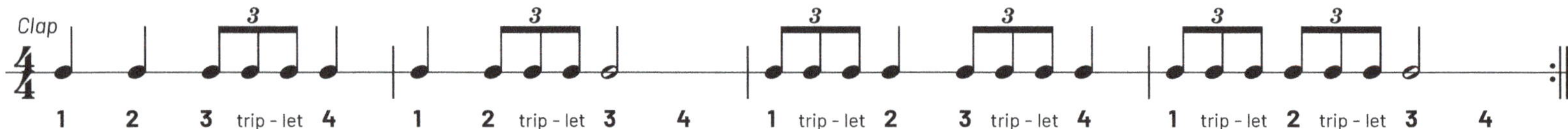

117. THREE TO GET READY

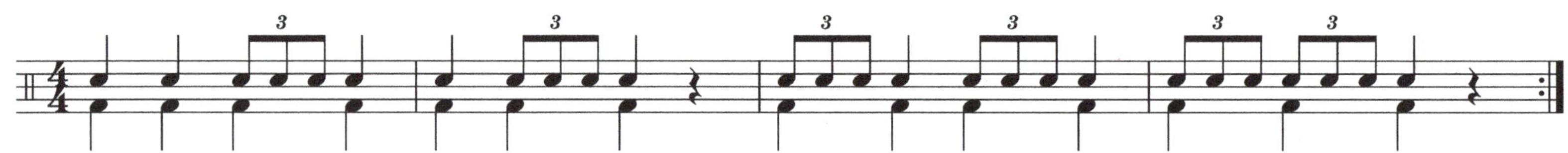

118. TRIPLET STUDY

119. MARCH (from THE NUTCRACKER) – Duet

Peter I. Tchaikovsky

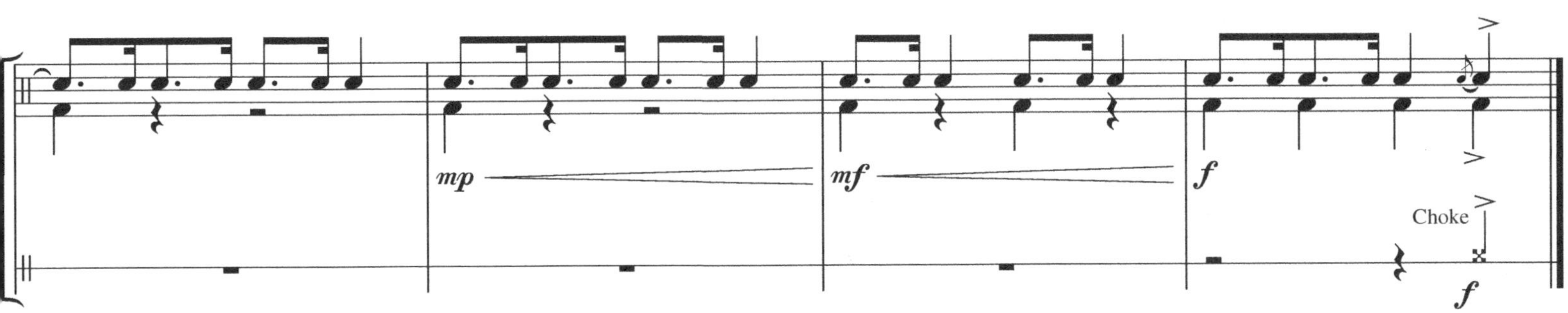

120. ESSENTIAL ELEMENTS QUIZ – THEME FROM FAUST

Charles Gounod

121. SCALE STUDY

122. OVER THE RIVER AND THROUGH THE WOODS

American Folk Song

123. RHYTHM RAP

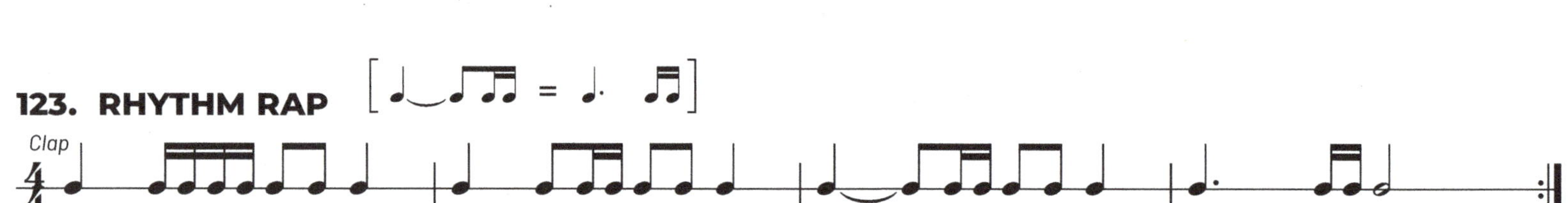

Hi-Hat

The hi-hat was introduced in the 1920's and is now a standard piece of equipment for the drum set. A small pair of cymbals are mounted on a stand, and a foot pedal allows the top cymbal to open and close on the bottom cymbal. The hi-hat is played with sticks with the cymbals in either a closed position or alternating between open and closed positions.

124. ON THE MOVE

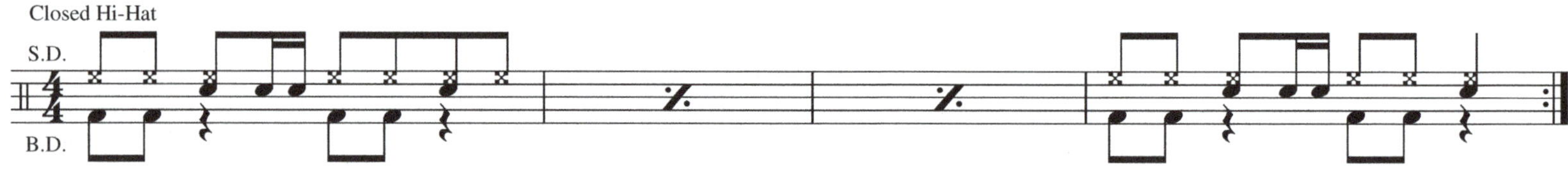

125. HIGHER GROUND

126. ESSENTIAL ELEMENTS QUIZ

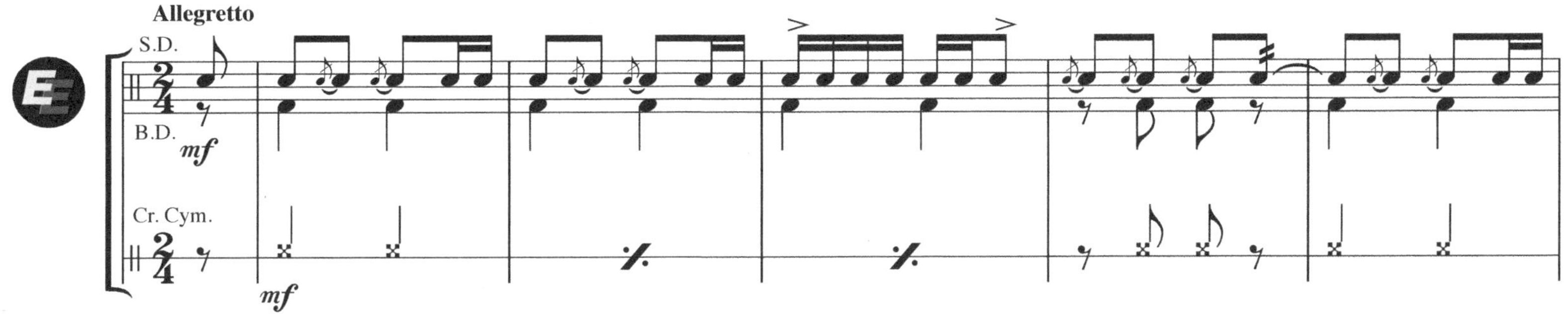

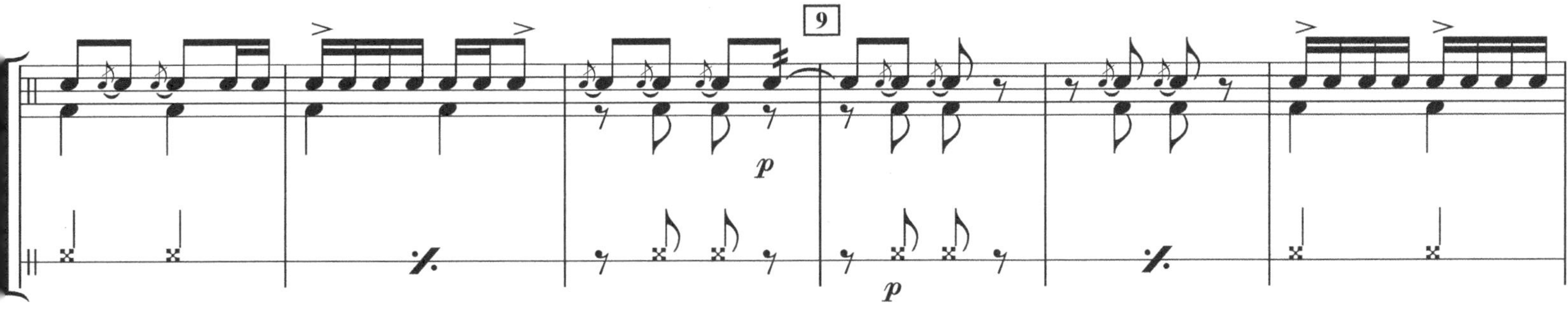

HISTORY

The first known printing of the lyrics and music to **The Marines' Hymn** dates from August 1, 1918. An unknown author is believed to have taken the opening words of the song from the words on the Marine Corps flag, "From the halls of Montezuma to the shores of Tripoli." The music was taken from "Genevieve de Brabant," by the operetta composer Jacques Offenbach.

127. THE MARINES' HYMN

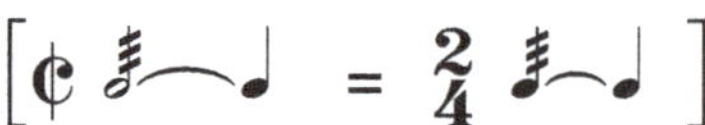

March Tempo

D.S. al Fine

Play until you see the **D.S. al Fine**. Then go back to the sign (𝄋) and play until the word **Fine**. **D.S.** is the abbreviation for **Dal Segno**, or "from the sign," and **Fine** means "the end."

128. D.S. MARCH

Accelerando *accel.* – Gradually faster.

129. CAN-CAN

Jacques Offenbach

129. CAN-CAN – Timpani

Jacques Offenbach

accel.

▲ *Watch your director.*

Natural Sticking

In order to obtain the proper feel when playing music in 6/8, percussionists often use natural sticking to enhance the phrasing. By applying an alternate sticking of R L R L R L to each measure, then remove the sticking when there is a rest, you are left with the natural sticking for the piece.

130. TARANTELLA

Italian Folk Song

HISTORY

The **waltz** is a dance in moderate 3/4 time which developed around 1800 from the Ländler, an Austrian peasant dance. Austrian composer **Johann Strauss, Jr.** (1825–1899) composed over 400 waltzes. These include such famous pieces as *The Blue Danube*, *Tales From the Vienna Woods* and *Emperor Waltz*.

131. EMPEROR WALTZ

Johann Strauss, Jr.

Andantino ◄ *Tempo between Andante and Moderato.*

Legato Style

legato – Wind players and kybd. perc. play in a smooth, connected style.

132. ENGLISH DANCE – Duet *Use natural sticking.*

Johann Christian Bach

133. ESSENTIAL ELEMENTS QUIZ – BRITISH GRENADIERS

Traditional

133. ESSENTIAL ELEMENTS QUIZ – BRITISH GRENADIERS – Timpani

Tune to F and C

Traditional

Congas

Congas are the largest hand drums in the Latin American percussion family. Traditionally, they are played as a single drum from a sitting position, but a double set of drums on a stand is also quite popular. While the Bongos use more of a finger technique, the Congas use the entire hand on the skin to produce the fullest sound. The printed hand motions will allow you to avoid crossing hands when you play.

134. NASSAU BOUND

Bahamian Folk Song

135. UNFINISHED SYMPHONY THEME

Franz Schubert

136. RHYTHM STUDY *Review flams, flam taps, and drags.*

137. COUNTRY GARDENS

English Folk Song

138. JOSHUA *Review doubling, or double sticking.*

African-American Spiritual

(Ex. 139)

Rudiment

Tap Flam

R R L L

The Tap Flam is simply the reverse of the rudiment Flam Tap. Notice once you get started, this new rudiment feels very much like the Flam Tap. The difference is that you begin this new rudiment with the tap stroke, followed by the flam.

139. LISTEN TO THE MOCKINGBIRD
Alice Hawthorne
Moderato
S.D.
B.D.
mf
Pick-up
Wd. Blk.
Sixteenth Note Triplets
= 1 beat
1 trip - let 2 trip - let
= 1/2 Beat
1 ah dah & ah dah
140. ANCHORS AWEIGH
Capt. A.H. Miles and C.A. Zimmerman
March Tempo
1 & ah dah 2
S.D.
B.D.
Cr. Cym.
cresc.

141. GREENSLEEVES

English Folk Song

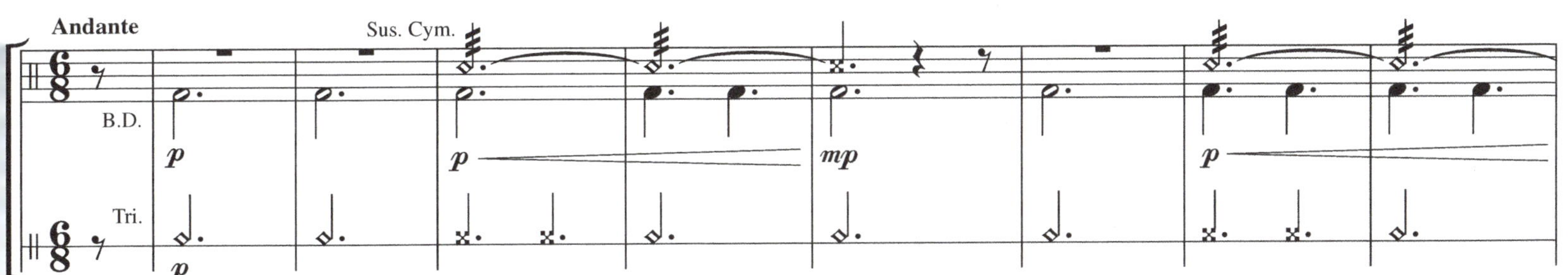

142. THE LONG CLIMB *Review paradiddle, triple paradiddle, double paradiddle*

143. THE BLUE BELLS OF SCOTLAND

Scottish Folk Song

Chimes Use a rawhide mallet or a special hammer with a synthetic head to play the chimes. There is a rounded cap that is placed at the top of each tube; this is the striking area. Always remember to play the instrument on the cap; *never* strike the instrument anywhere else or you will damage the tubes.

143. THE BLUE BELLS OF SCOTLAND – Chimes

Scottish Folk Song

THEORY

Major and Minor

The scales you've already learned are called **Major** scales. They all follow the same pattern, with **half-steps** between notes 3-4 and between notes 7-8.

Natural Minor scales follow a different pattern, with **half-steps** between notes 2-3 and 5-6. The **G Minor** scale uses the same key signature as **B♭ Major**.

Another type of minor scale is called **Harmonic Minor**, which adds an accidental to raise the **7th** note by a half-step. Compare the scales on the right.

Winds and kybd. perc. have additional minor scales on p. 37.

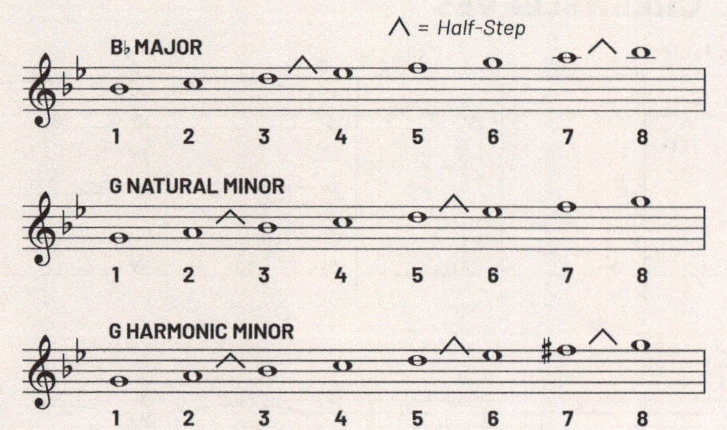

144. NATURAL MINOR SCALE

145. FINALE FROM "NEW WORLD SYMPHONY"

Antonin Dvorák

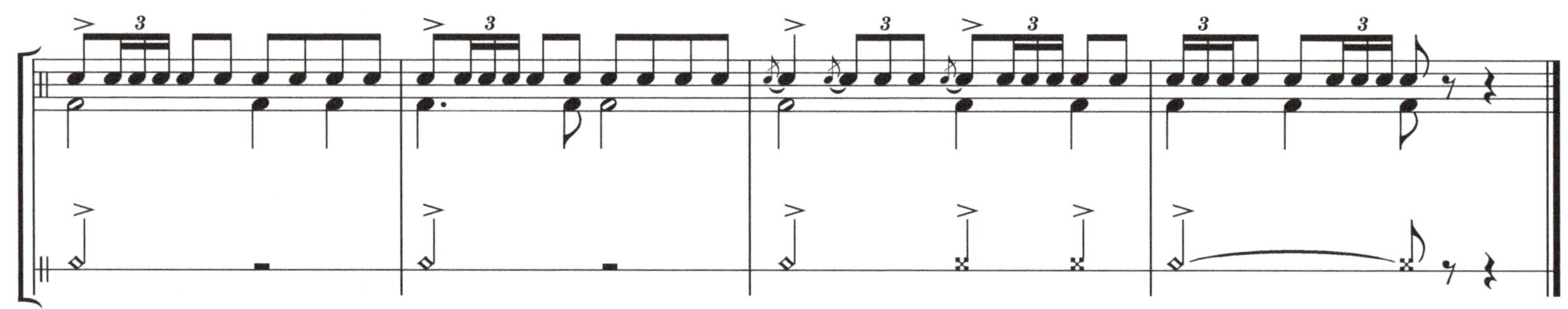

146. HARMONIC MINOR SCALE

147. HUNGARIAN DANCE NO. 5

Johannes Brahms

148. POMP AND CIRCUMSTANCE (LAND OF HOPE AND GLORY)

Edward Elgar

PERFORMANCE SPOTLIGHT

D.S. al Coda Play until you see the **D.S. al Coda**. Then go back to the sign (𝄋) and play until the **Coda Sign** ("To Coda" ⊕). Skip directly to the **Coda** and play until the end.

Open Rolls in 6/8

Use eighth note hand motions and play double bounces on the rolls.

150. SEMPER FIDELIS – Band Arrangement

Snare Drum, Bass Drum

John Philip Sousa
Arr. by John Higgins

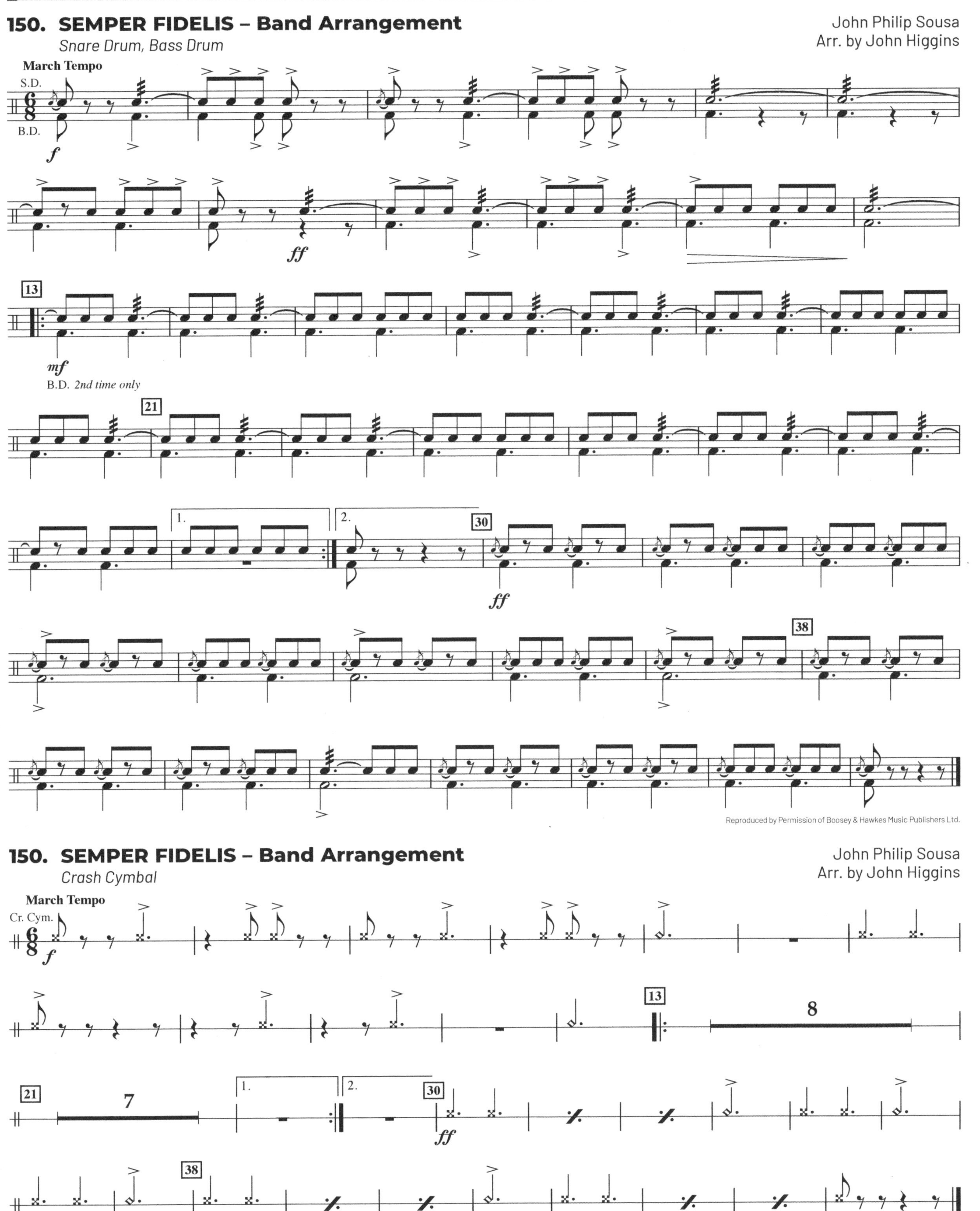

PERFORMANCE SPOTLIGHT

151. DANNY BOY – Band Arrangement

Snare Drum, Bass Drum

Irish Folk Song
Arr. by John Higgins

151. DANNY BOY – Band Arrangement

Triangle, Sus. Cym.

Irish Folk Song
Arr. by John Higgins

152. TAKE ME OUT TO THE BALL GAME – Band Arrangement

Snare Drum, Bass Drum

By Jack Norworth and Harry von Tilzer
Arr. by John Higgins

Allegretto

S.D.
B.D.

f

Play on Rim

5

mf

13

Play on Rim

mp

21

Play on Rim

mf

29

ff

1.

2.

152. TAKE ME OUT TO THE BALL GAME – Band Arrangement

Wd. Blk., Tri., Cr. Cym.

By Jack Norworth and Harry von Tilzer
Arr. by John Higgins

Allegretto

Wd. Blk.

f

5

8

13

Tri.

mp

Cr. Cym.

f

21

Wd. Blk.

mf

29

Cr. Cym.

ff

4

1.

Choke

2.

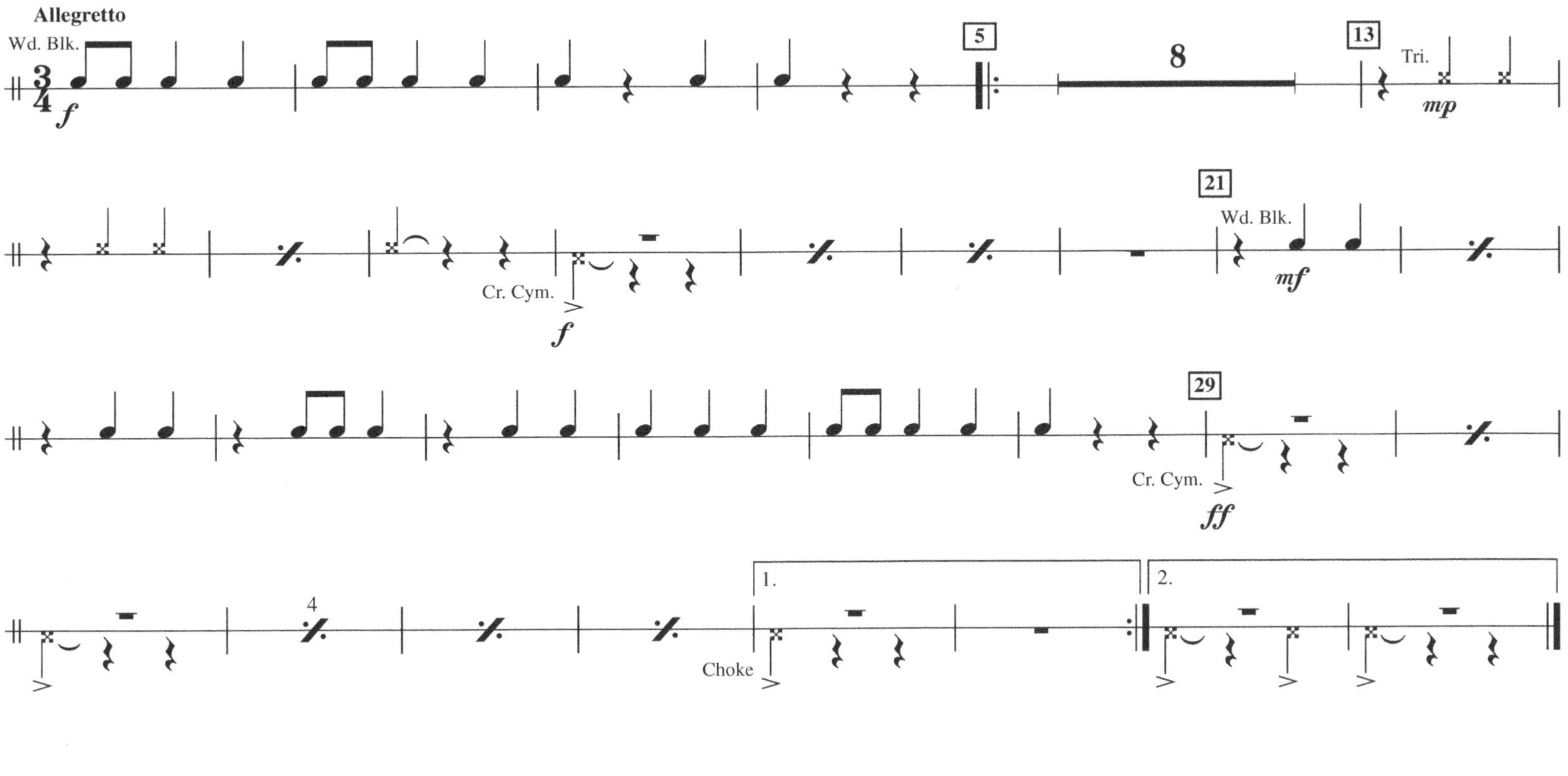

PERFORMANCE SPOTLIGHT

153. SERENGETI (AFRICAN RHAPSODY) – Band Arrangement

John Higgins

Bass Drum, Tom-Toms, Guiro, Bongos

Wind Chimes

Wind Chimes are varying lengths of a brass or metal alloy hung from a short wooden bar. They are played by gently sweeping the hand along the line of strung tubes, generally from the high to low end.

153. SERENGETI (AFRICAN RHAPSODY) – Band Arrangement

John Higgins

Wind Chimes, Sus. Cym., Shaker, Cowbell, Triangle

RUBANK® STUDIES

154. CHORALE

154. CHORALE – Timpani

Tune to F and B♭

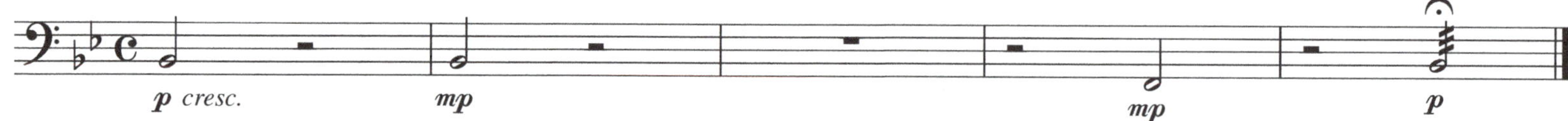

155. CHORALE

155. CHORALE – Timpani

Tune to B♭ and E♭

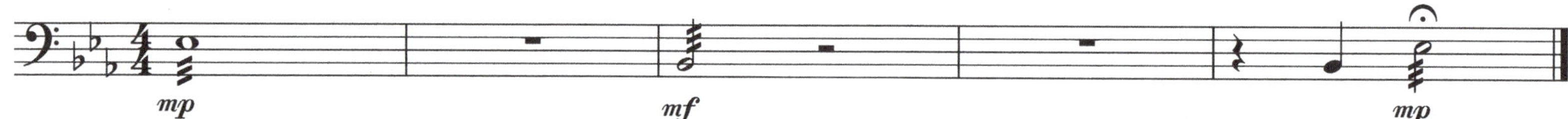

156. CHORALE

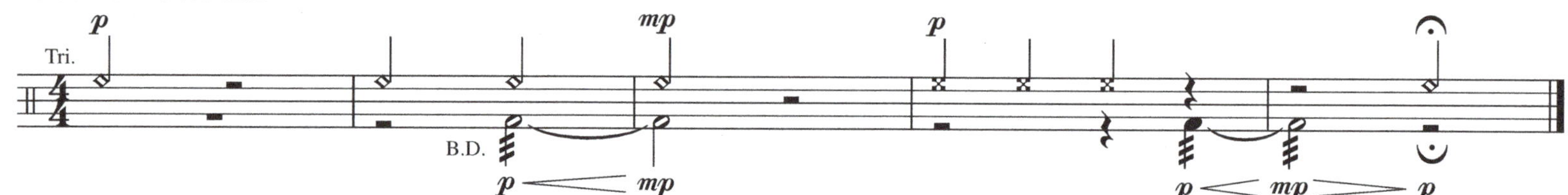

156. CHORALE – Timpani

Tune to F and C

157. CHORALE

157. CHORALE – Timpani

Tune to A♭ and E♭

158. CHORALE

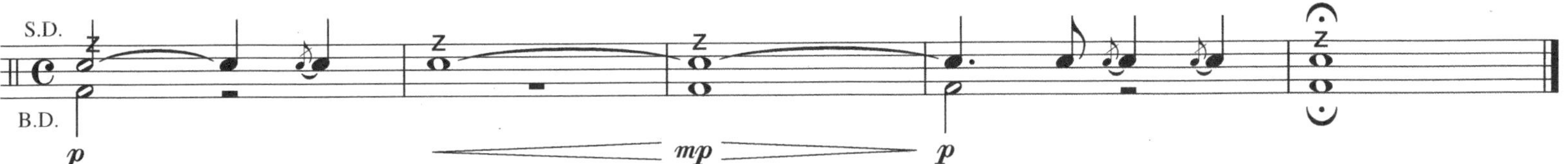

KEY OF B♭

159.

160.

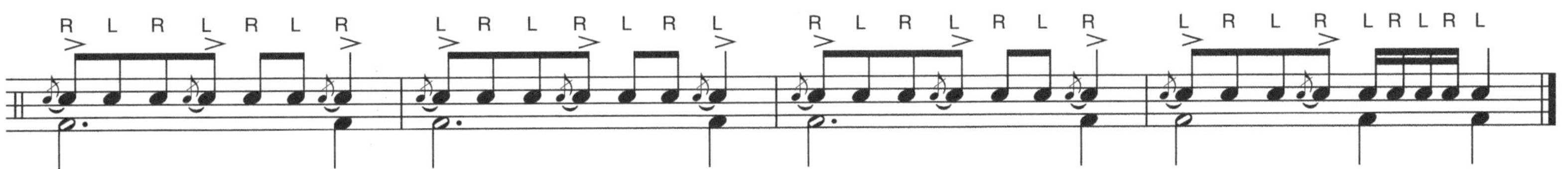

161.

162.

RUBANK® STUDIES

KEY OF E♭

163.

164.

165.

166.

KEY OF F

167.

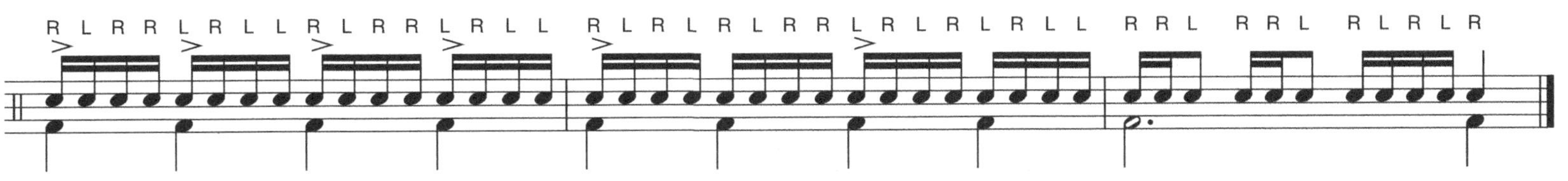

168.

169.

170.

RUBANK® STUDIES

KEY OF A♭

171.

172.

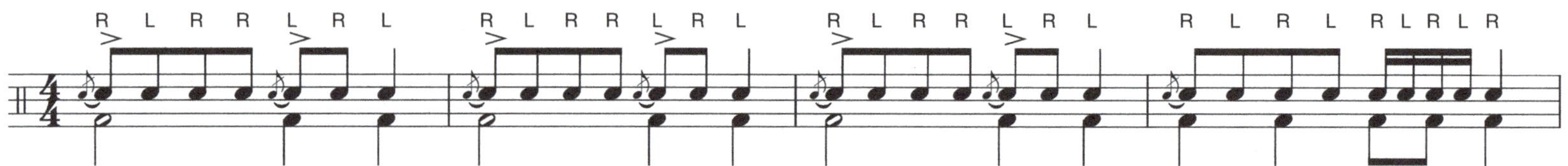

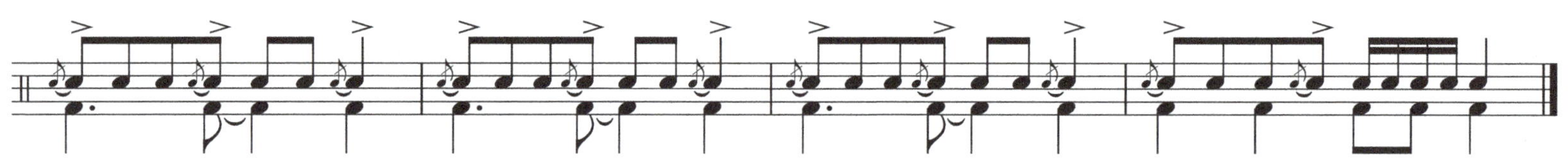

173.

174.

KEY OF C

RUBANK® STUDIES

KEY OF G MINOR

179.

180.

KEY OF C MINOR

181.

182.

KEY OF D MINOR

183.

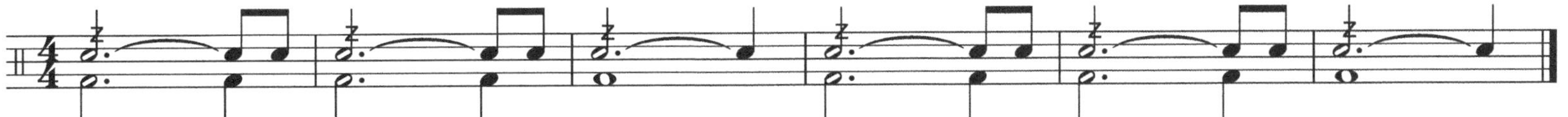

184.

CHROMATIC SCALES

185.

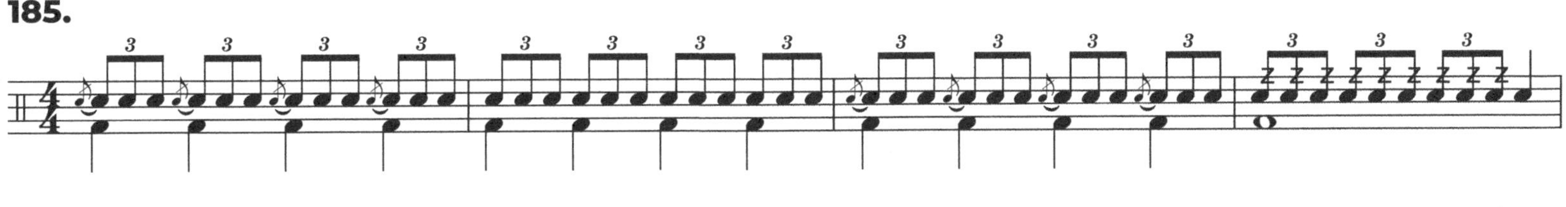

186.

INDIVIDUAL STUDY – Percussion

187. SNARE DRUM – TRIPLET BASED MULTIPLE BOUNCE ROLL EXERCISE #1

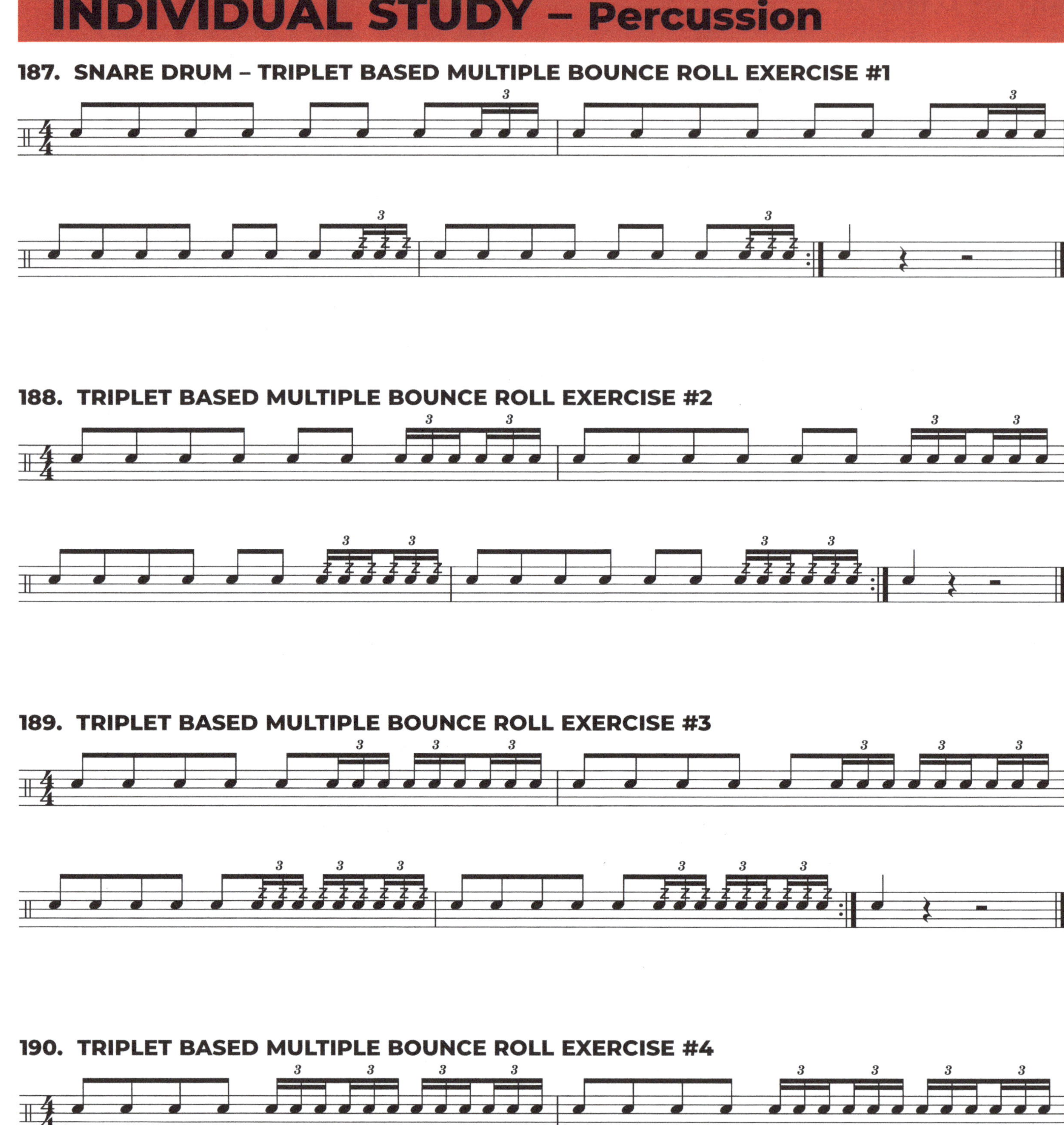

188. TRIPLET BASED MULTIPLE BOUNCE ROLL EXERCISE #2

189. TRIPLET BASED MULTIPLE BOUNCE ROLL EXERCISE #3

190. TRIPLET BASED MULTIPLE BOUNCE ROLL EXERCISE #4

191. FLAM ACCENT #1 – FLAM ACCENT #2 COMBINATION

192. FLAMADIDDLE, FLAM TAP, PATAFLAFLA, FLAMACUE COMBINATION

193. MEASURED ROLL COMBINATION – Alternating 5, 9, 13, and 17 Stroke Rolls

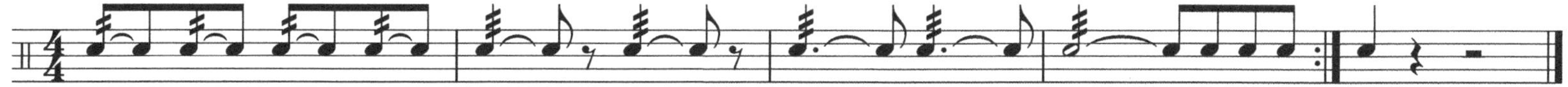

194. MEASURED ROLL COMBINATION – Non Alternating 7, 11, and 15 Stroke Rolls

INDIVIDUAL STUDY – Percussion

195. BASS DRUM ETUDE

196. CRASH CYMBAL STUDY

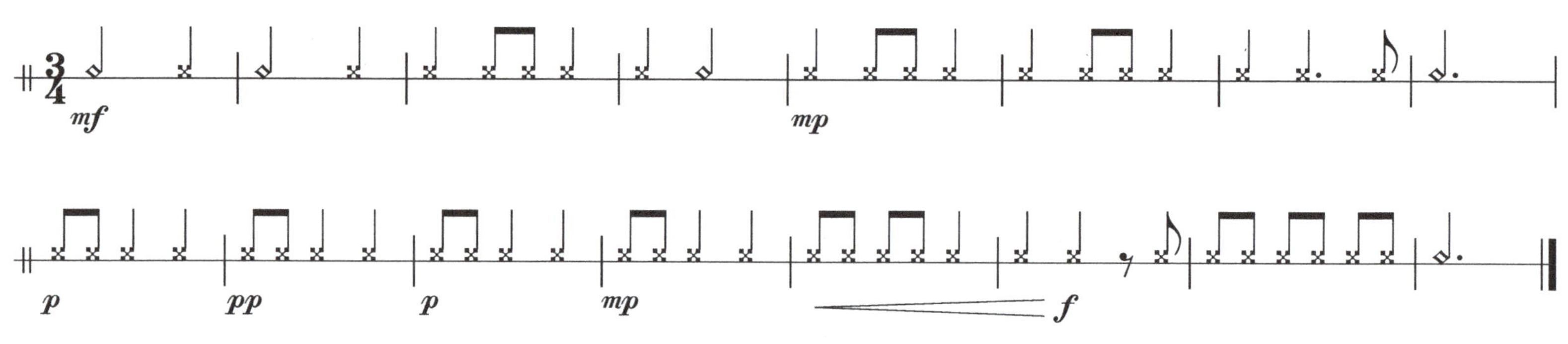

197. TAMBOURINE ETUDE

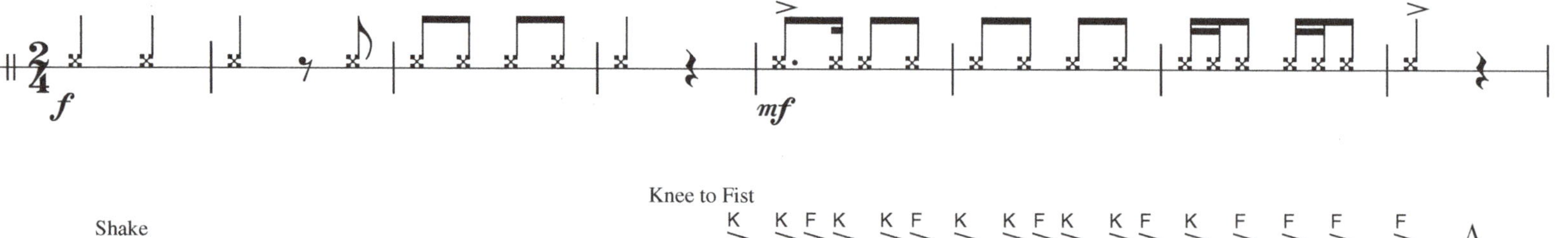

198. TRIANGLE STUDY

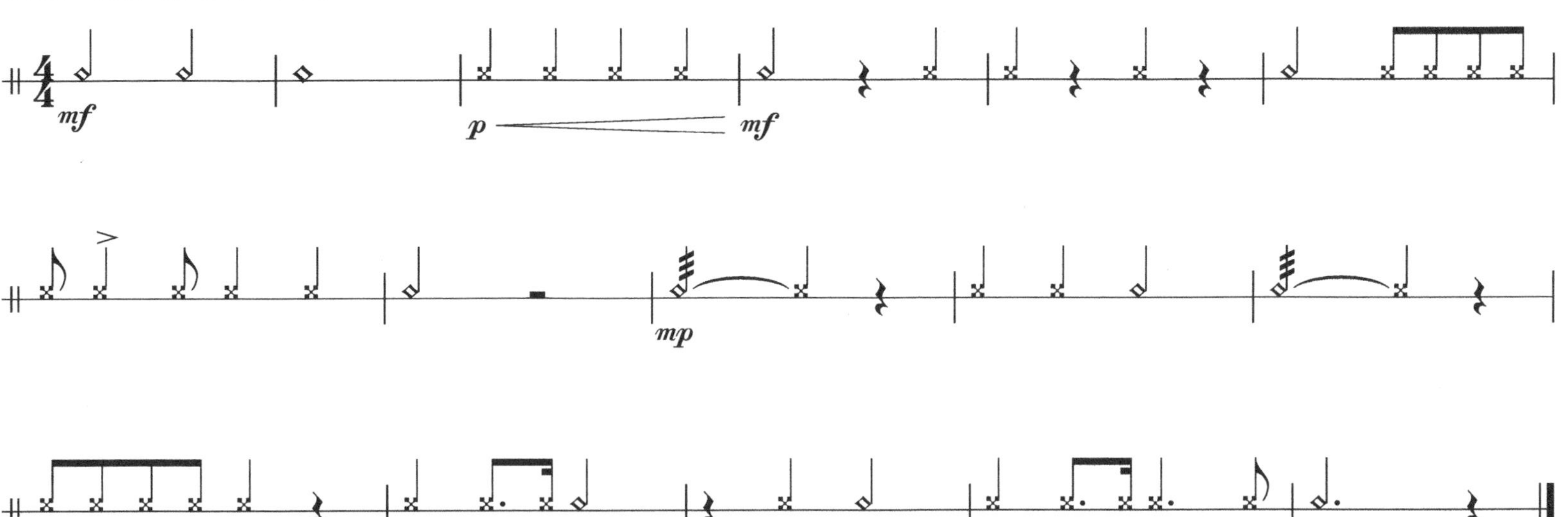

199. TIMPANI ETUDE

Tune to A and D

INDIVIDUAL STUDY – Percussion

200. ACCENT ARTICULATO – Snare Drum Solo (Unaccompanied)

Will Rapp

Online audio – see inside front cover to access.

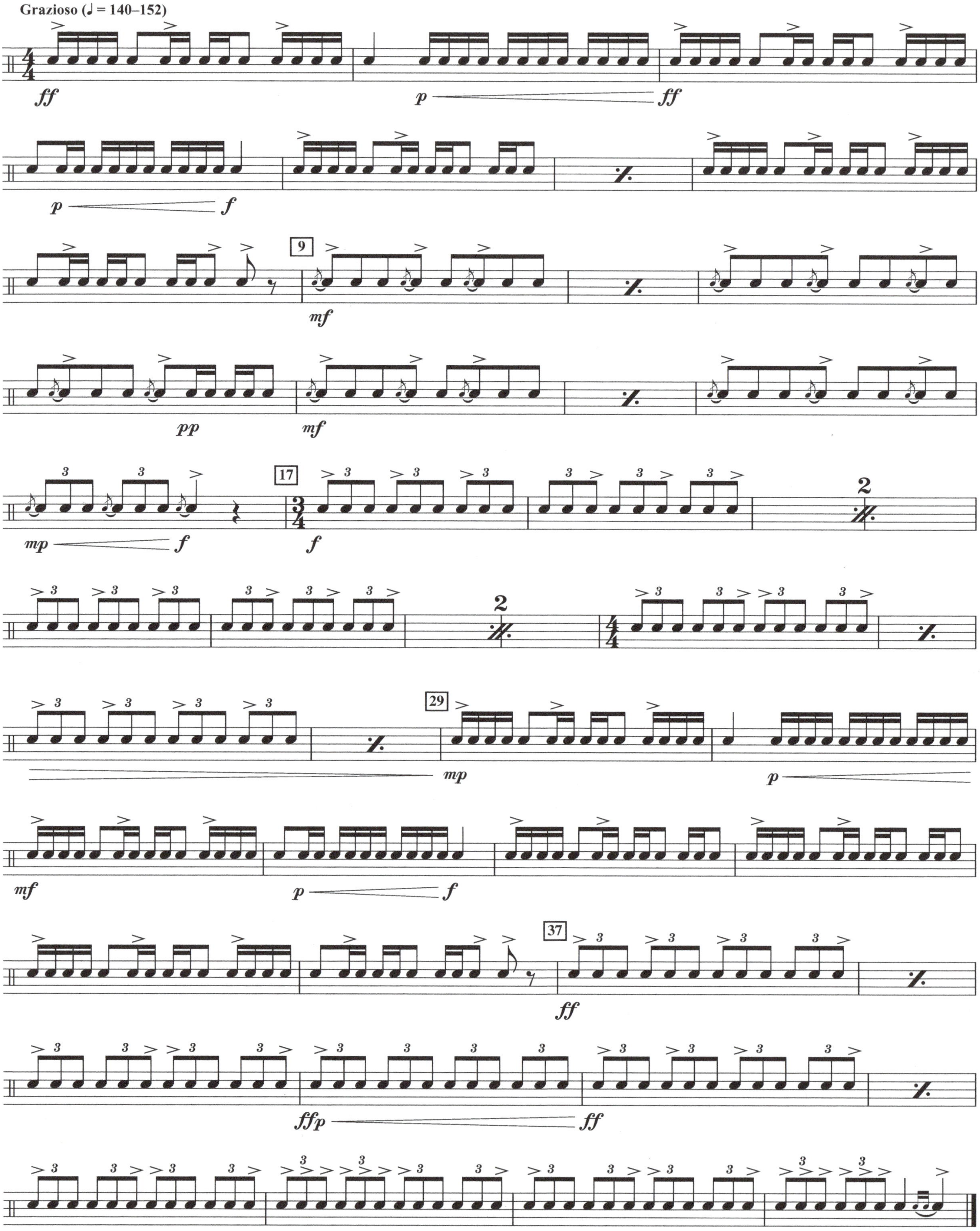

Grazioso (♩ = 140–152)

ff p ff p f 9 mf pp mf mp f 17 f 2 2 29 mp p mf p f 37 ff ffp ff

INDIVIDUAL STUDY – Percussion

201. STRAIGHT SIX EIGHT – Snare Drum Solo (Unaccompanied)

Will Rapp

Online audio – see inside front cover to access.

RHYTHM STUDIES

RHYTHM STUDIES

CREATING MUSIC

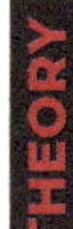

THEORY

Theme and Variation

Theme and Variation is a technique used by composers and arrangers to create interesting musical ideas that are "varied" from an established melody, or "theme." Play the following theme and two variations on kybd. perc. to hear how the arranger has created new phrases based on the original melody.

1. THEME

"Simple Gifts"

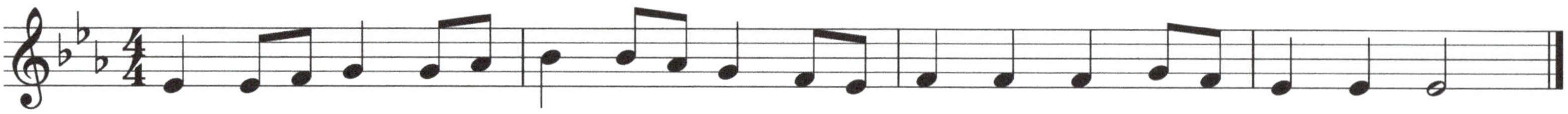

VARIATION 1 *Adding some notes • Changing some rhythms*

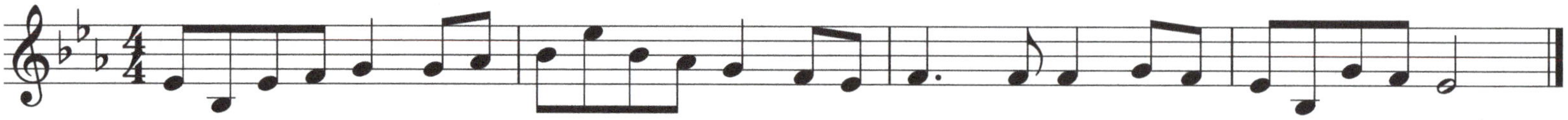

VARIATION 2 *Removing notes • Changing rhythms • Adding accents • Adding notes*

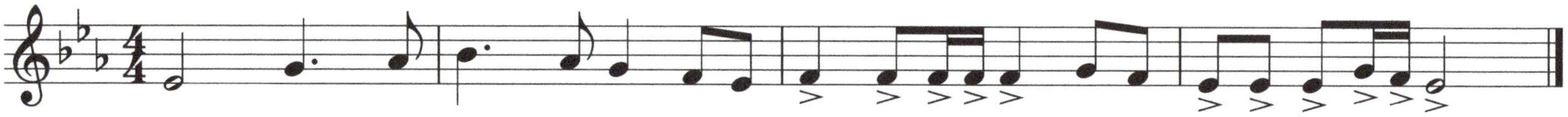

2. THEME AND YOUR VARIATION

Write your own variation of this theme. Use your instrument to hear and try different ideas.

"Candy Mountain Rock"

Theme

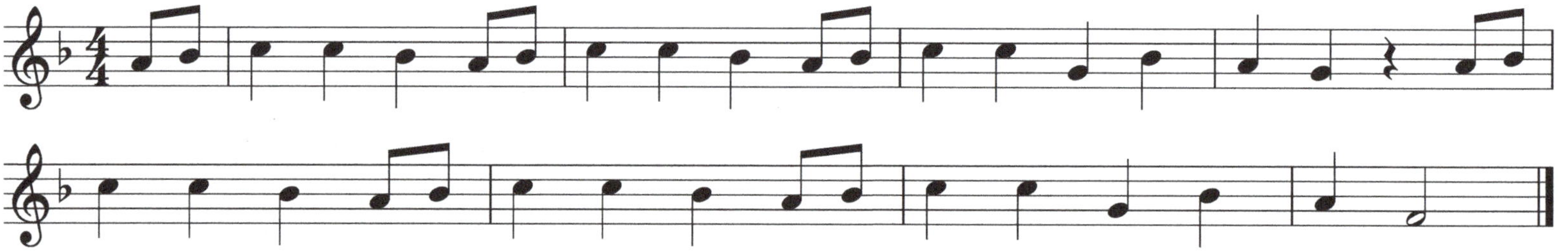

Your Variation

THEORY

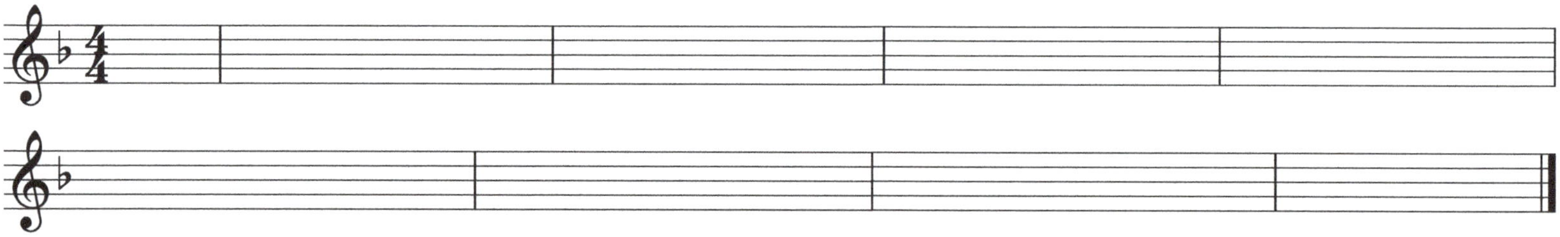

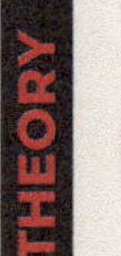

Blues Improvisation

Improvisation using a **Blues Scale** is an important part of jazz and popular music. Musicians use combinations of these notes and various rhythms to create their own spontaneous solos over a 12 measure progression of chords.

Blues Scale

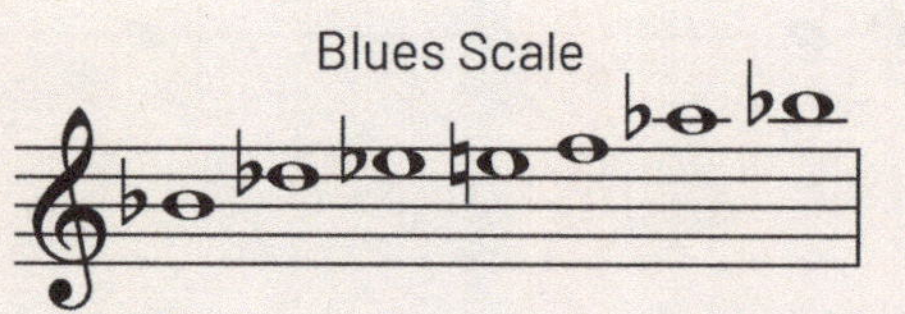

3. LET'S JAM

Use the indicated notes from the Blues Scale to create your own solo to play with the accompaniment (Line B).

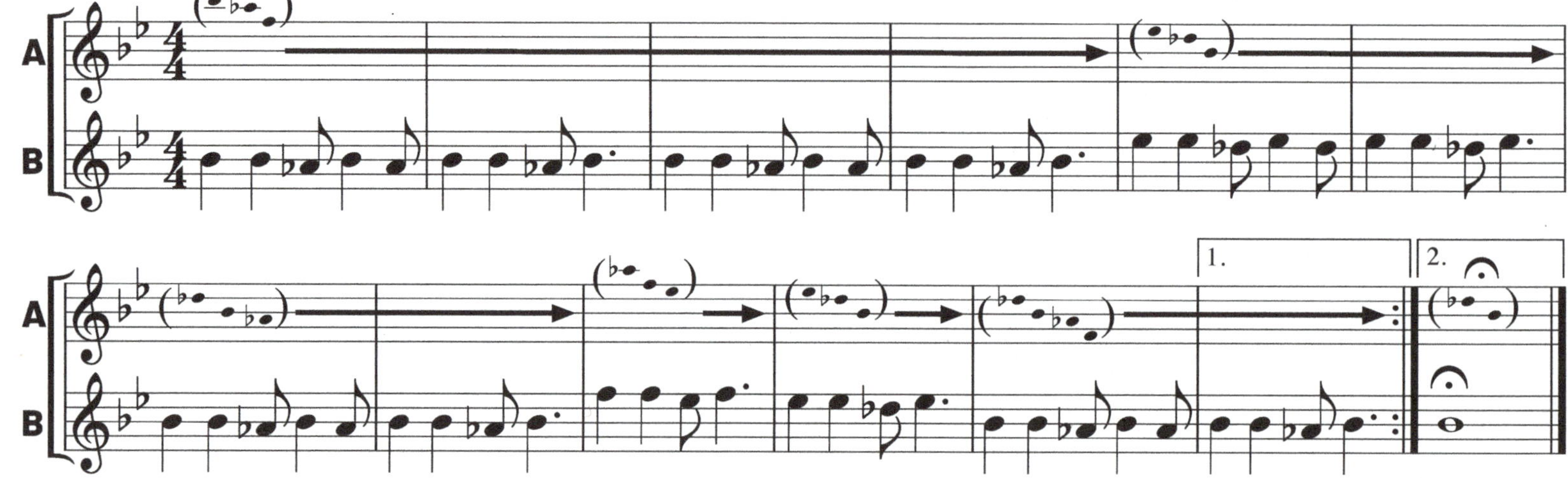

You can mark your progress through the book on this page.
Fill in the stars as instructed by your band director.

1. Page 2–4, Review
2. Page 5, Sightreading Challenge, No. 19
3. Page 6, Daily Warm-Ups
4. Page 7, Sightreading Challenge, No. 31
5. Page 8, Essential Creativity, No. 38
6. Page 9, EE Quiz, No. 43
7. Page 10, Sightreading Challenge, No. 49
8. Page 11, EE Quiz, No. 55
9. Page 12–13, Performance Spotlight
10. Page 15, EE Quiz, No. 74
11. Page 16, Sightreading Challenge, No. 80
12. Page 18, Daily Warm-Ups
13. Page 19, Essential Creativity, No. 96
14. Page 20, Sightreading Challenge, No. 100
15. Page 21, EE Quiz, No. 106
16. Page 22, Chromatic Scale, No. 107
17. Page 23, Sightreading Challenge, No. 115
18. Page 24, EE Quiz, No. 120
19. Page 25, EE Quiz, No. 126
20. Page 27, EE Quiz, No. 133
21. Page 30, Natural Minor Scale, No. 144
22. Page 30, Harmonic Minor Scale, No. 146
23. Page 30, Pomp and Circumstance, No. 148
24. Page 31, Performance Spotlight
25. Page 32, Performance Spotlight
26. Page 33, Performance Spotlight
27. Page 38–39, Individual Study
28. Page 40, Performance Spotlight

MUSIC — AN ESSENTIAL ELEMENT OF LIFE

SNARE DRUM INTERNATIONAL DRUM RUDIMENTS

All rudiments should be practiced: open (slow) or close (fast) and/or at an even moderate march tempo.

Instrument Care Reminders

Snare drums occasionally need tuning. Ask your teacher to help you tighten each tension rod equally using a drum key.

- Be careful not to over-tighten the head. It will break if the tension is too tight.
- Loosen the snare strainer at the end of each rehearsal.
- Cover all percussion instruments when not in use.
- Put sticks away in a storage area. Keep the percussion section neat!
- Sticks are the only things which should be placed on the snare drum. NEVER put or allow others to put objects on any percussion instrument.

Instruments and photos courtesy of Yamaha.

I. ROLL RUDIMENTS

A. SINGLE STROKE RUDIMENTS

1. Single Stroke Roll

2. Single Stroke Four

3. Single Stroke Seven

B. MULTIPLE BOUNCE ROLL RUDIMENTS

4. Multiple Bounce Roll

5. Triple Stroke Roll

International Drum Rudiments courtesy of Percussion Arts Society

SNARE DRUM INTERNATIONAL DRUM RUDIMENTS

C. DOUBLE STROKE OPEN ROLL RUDIMENTS

6. Double Stroke Open Roll

11. Ten Stroke Roll

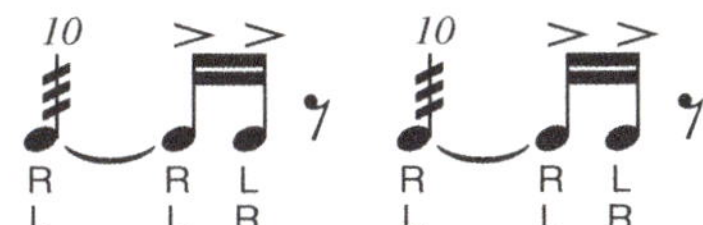

7. Five Stroke Roll

12. Eleven Stroke Roll

8. Six Stroke Roll

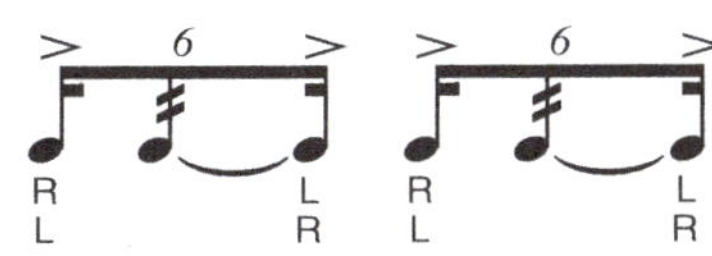

13. Twelve Stroke Roll

9. Seven Stroke Roll

14. Fifteen Stroke Roll

10. Nine Stroke Roll

15. Seventeen Stroke Roll

II. DIDDLE RUDIMENTS

16. Single Paradiddle

18. Triple Paradiddle

17. Double Paradiddle

19. Single Paradiddle-Diddle

SNARE DRUM INTERNATIONAL DRUM RUDIMENTS

III. FLAM RUDIMENTS

20. Flam

21. Flam Accent

22. Flam Tap

23. Flamacue

24. Flam Paradiddle (Flamadiddle)

25. Single Flammed Mill

26. Flam Paradiddle-Diddle

27. Pataflafla

28. Swiss Army Triplet

29. Inverted Flam Tap

30. Flam Drag

IV. DRAG RUDIMENTS

31. Drag

32. Single Drag Tap

33. Double Drag Tap

34. Lesson 25

35. Single Dragadiddle

36. Drag Paradiddle #1

37. Drag Paradiddle #2

38. Single Ratamacue

38. Double Ratamacue

40. Triple Ratamacue

Reference Index

Definitions (pg.)

Book 1 Review

Composers

World Music

Reference Index for Percussion

Definitions (pg.)

*These page numbers refer to the first section (percussion) of this book.

KEYBOARD PERCUSSION BOOK 2

ESSENTIAL ELEMENTS for Band

Bonus **Popular Songs** Online

COMPREHENSIVE BAND METHOD

TIM LAUTZENHEISER
JOHN HIGGINS
CHARLES MENGHINI
PAUL LAVENDER
TOM C. RHODES
DON BIERSCHENK

Percussion consultant and editor
WILL RAPP

HAL•LEONARD®

ESSENTIAL ELEMENTS for Band

COMPREHENSIVE BAND METHOD

TIM LAUTZENHEISER • JOHN HIGGINS • CHARLES MENGHINI
PAUL LAVENDER • TOM C. RHODES • DON BIERSCHENK

Percussion consultant and editor
WILL RAPP

ISBN 979-835013691-3

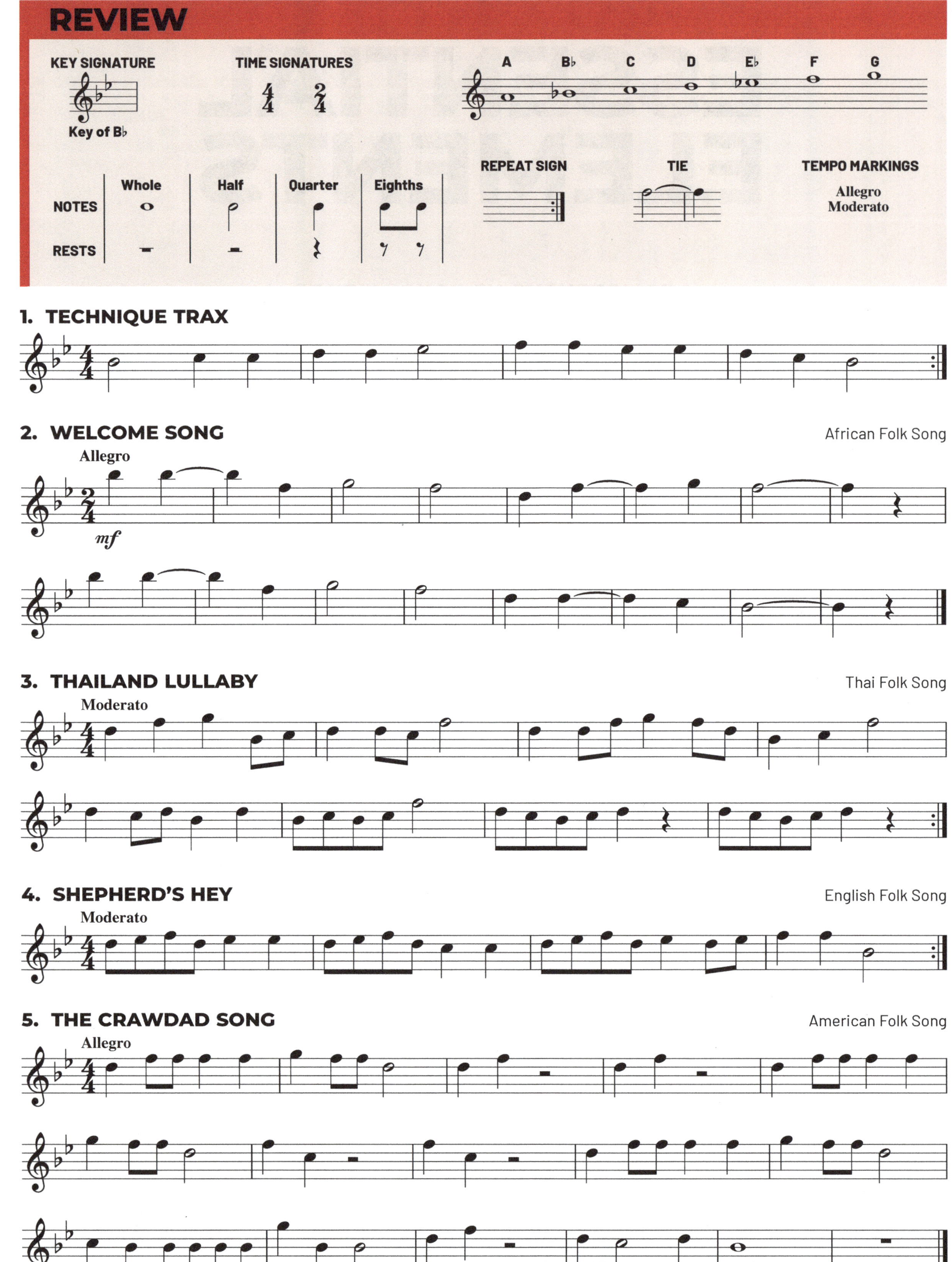
REVIEW
KEY SIGNATURE
Key of B♭
TIME SIGNATURES
A
B♭
C
D
E♭
F
G
Whole
Half
Quarter
Eighths
NOTES
RESTS
REPEAT SIGN
TIE
TEMPO MARKINGS
Allegro
Moderato
1. TECHNIQUE TRAX
2. WELCOME SONG
African Folk Song
Allegro
mf
3. THAILAND LULLABY
Thai Folk Song
Moderato
4. SHEPHERD'S HEY
English Folk Song
Moderato
5. THE CRAWDAD SONG
American Folk Song
Allegro

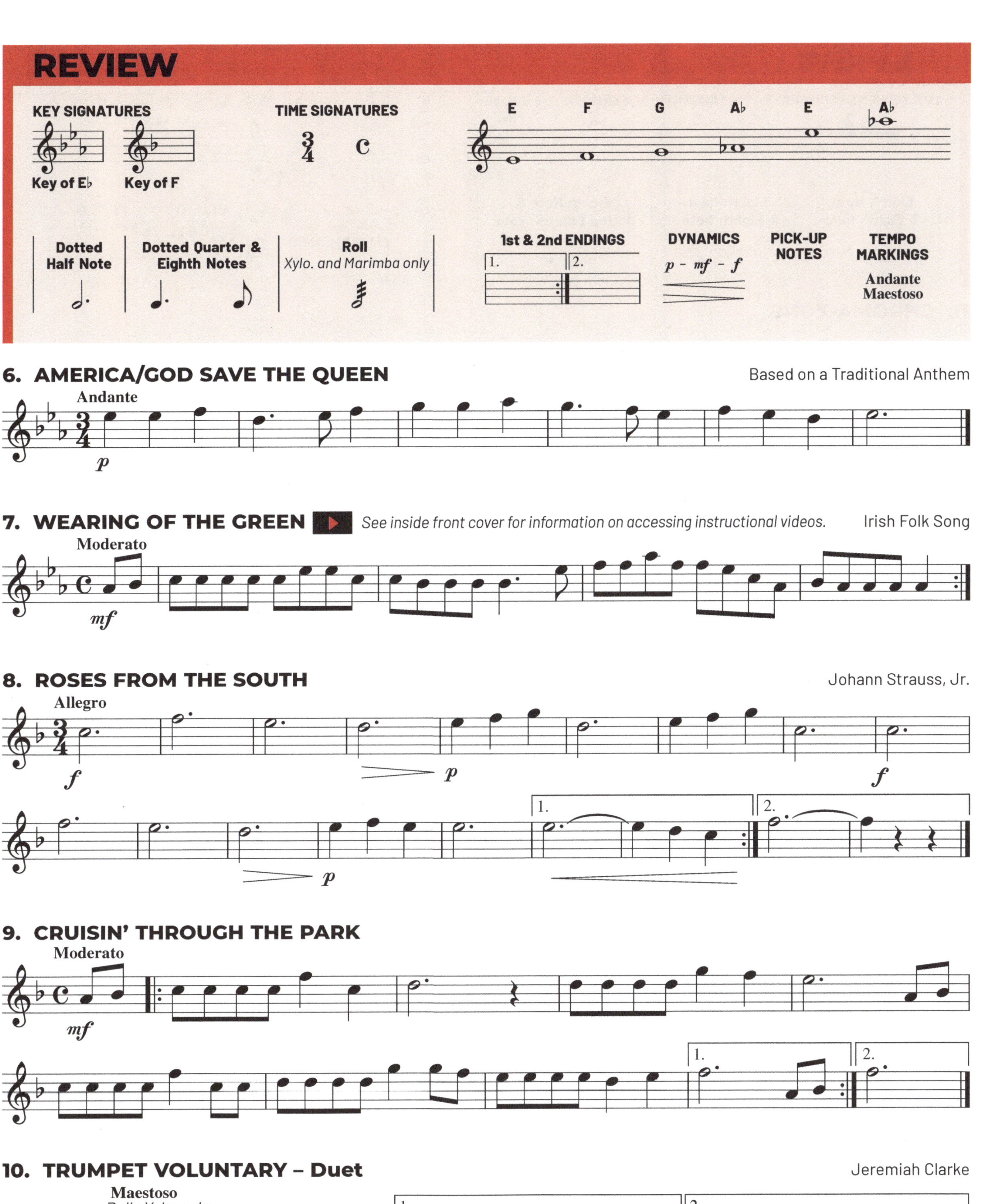
REVIEW
KEY SIGNATURES
Key of E♭
Key of F
TIME SIGNATURES
E
F
G
A♭
E
A♭
Dotted Half Note
Dotted Quarter & Eighth Notes
Roll
Xylo. and Marimba only
1st & 2nd ENDINGS
1.
2.
DYNAMICS
p - mf - f
PICK-UP NOTES
TEMPO MARKINGS
Andante
Maestoso
6. AMERICA/GOD SAVE THE QUEEN
Based on a Traditional Anthem
Andante
p
7. WEARING OF THE GREEN
See inside front cover for information on accessing instructional videos.
Irish Folk Song
Moderato
mf
8. ROSES FROM THE SOUTH
Johann Strauss, Jr.
Allegro
f
p
f
1.
2.
p
9. CRUISIN' THROUGH THE PARK
Moderato
mf
1.
2.
10. TRUMPET VOLUNTARY – Duet
Jeremiah Clarke
Maestoso
Rolls Xylo. only
1.
2.
A
B
f
f

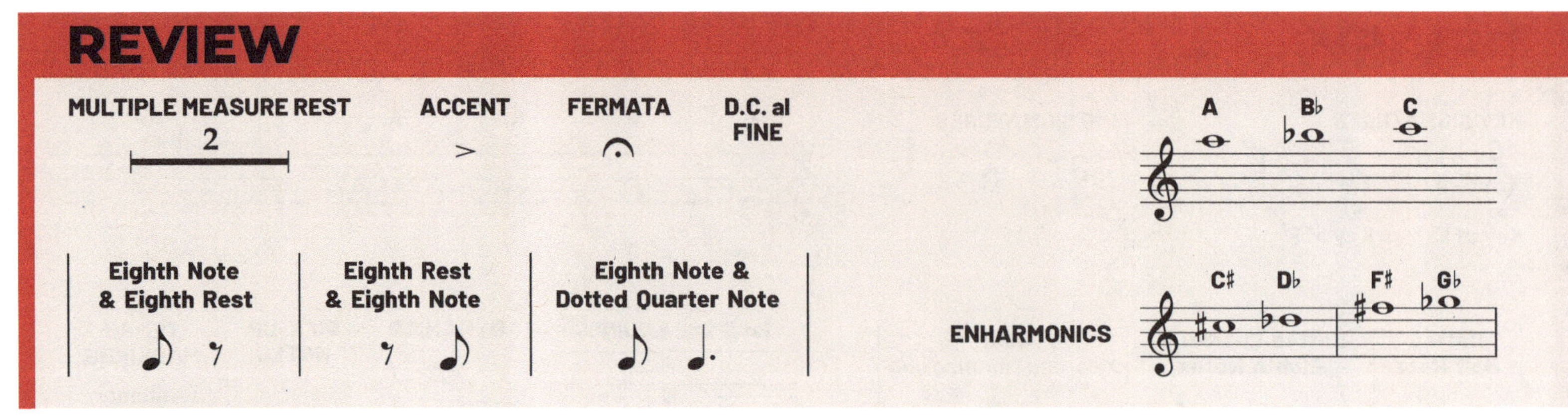

11. CHROMA-ZONE

mf · Fine · 2 · D.C. al Fine · *f*

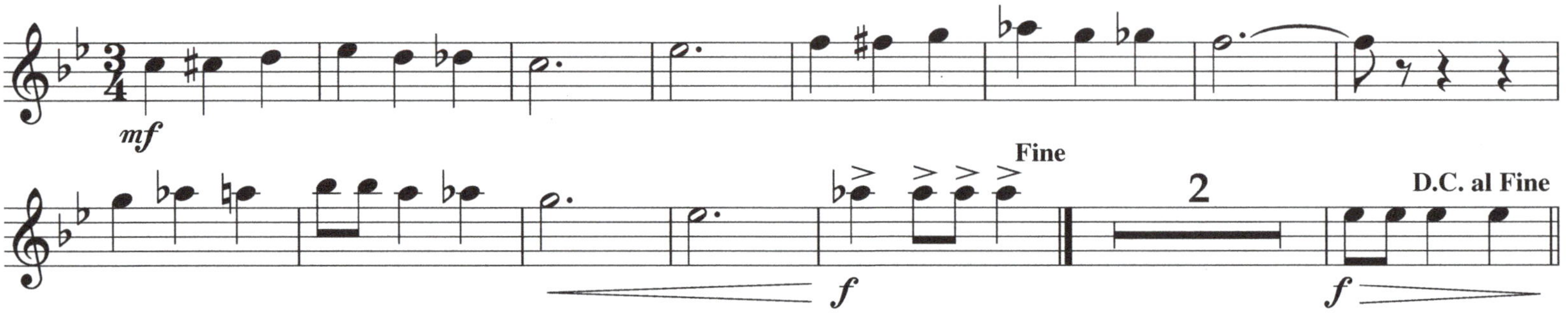

12. BILLY BOY

American Folk Song

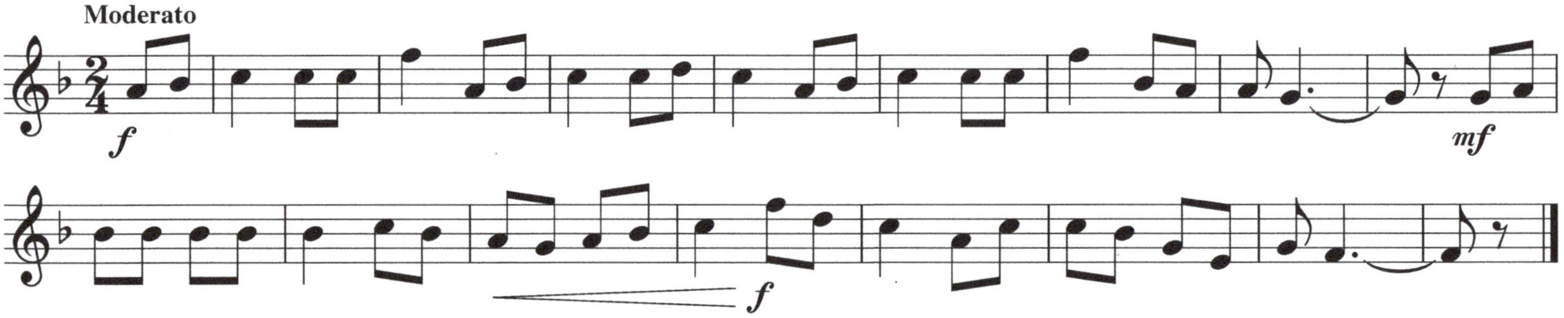

Moderato

f · *mf* · *f*

13. TECHNIQUE TRAX

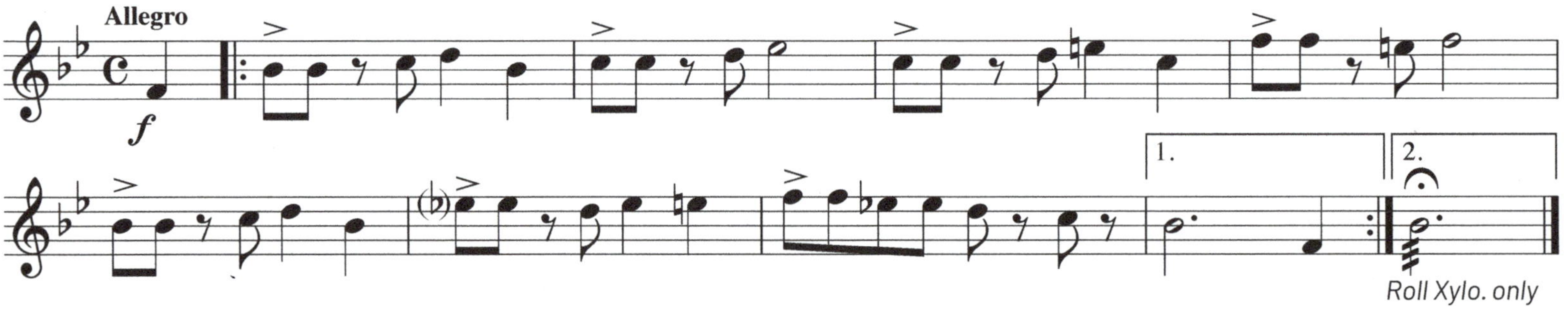

Allegro

f · 1. · 2.

Roll Xylo. only

14. SALSA SIESTA – Duet

Staccato

For woodwind and brass players, staccato notes are played lightly and with separation. They are marked with a dot above or below the note.

15. TREADING LIGHTLY

Tenuto

For woodwind and brass players, tenuto notes are played smoothly and connected, without any break. They are marked with a straight line above or below the note.

16. SMOOTH MOVE

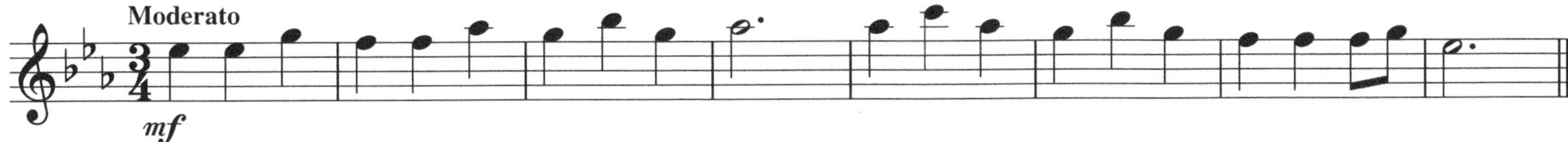

17. SHIFTING GEARS

HISTORY

English composer **Thomas Tallis** (1508–1585) served as a royal court composer for Kings Henry VIII and Edward VI, and Queens Mary and Elizabeth. During Tallis' lifetime, the artist Michelangelo painted the Sistine Chapel.

Canons (one or more parts imitating the first part) were used in many forms by 16th century composers. A **Round** is a strict (or exact) canon which can be repeated any number of times without stopping. Play *Tallis Canon* as a 4-part round.

18. TALLIS CANON (Round)

Thomas Tallis

Sightreading

Sightreading means playing a musical piece for the first time. The key to sightreading success is to know what to look for *before* you play. Use the word **S-T-A-R-S** to remind yourself what to look for, and eventually your band will become sightreading STARS!

- **S** – **Sharps or flats** in the key signature
- **T** – **Time signature** and **tempo markings**
- **A** – **Accidentals** not found in the key signature
- **R** – **Rhythms**, silently counting the more difficult notes and rests
- **S** – **Signs**, including dynamics, articulations, repeats and endings

19. SIGHTREADING CHALLENGE

DAILY WARM-UPS

WORK-OUTS FOR TONE & TECHNIQUE

20. TONE BUILDER

Rolls Xylo. only

21. FLEXIBILITY STUDY

22. TECHNIQUE TRAX

23. CHORALE

Johann Sebastian Bach

Andante

p

mf

p

24. GRANDFATHER'S CLOCK

Henry C. Work

Ritardando *ritard.* (or) *rit.* – Gradually slower.

25. GLOW WORM

Paul Lincke

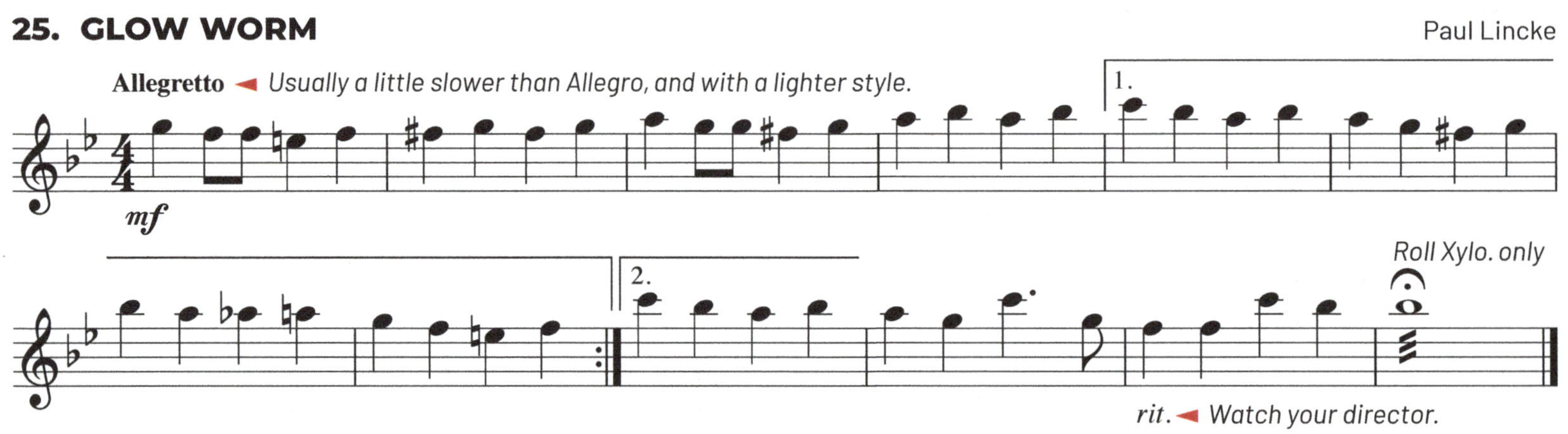

26. ALMA MATER

A.C. Weekes, W.M. Smith, H.S. Thompson

HISTORY

The Scottish folk song *Loch Lomond* is credited to an anonymous soldier who was imprisoned and awaiting execution. In it he writes of his desire to return home to his family and the breathtaking beauty of Loch (Lake) Lomond, a lake in Scotland. Located in the southern highlands, the lake is almost entirely surrounded by hills. One of these is Ben Lomond, a peak 3,192 feet high.

27. LOCH LOMOND

Scottish Folk Song

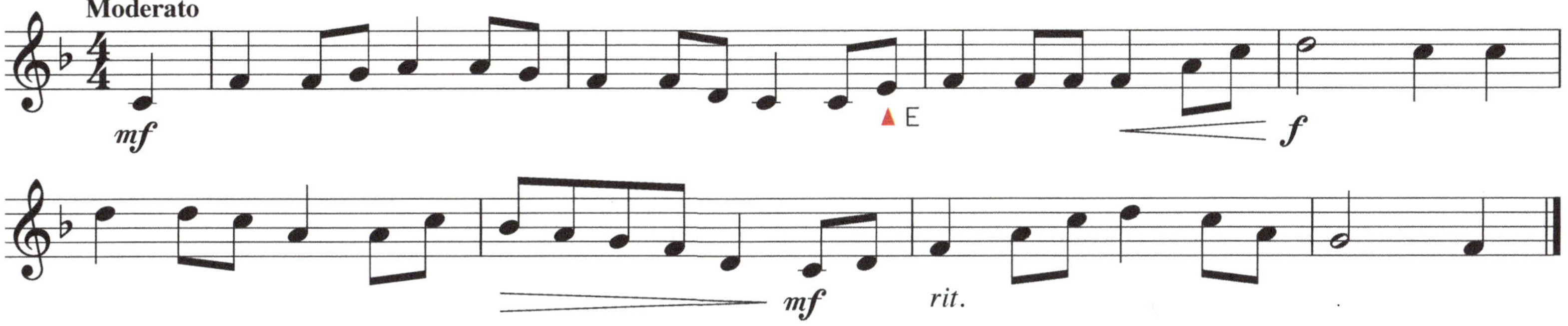

THEORY

Key Changes

If a key signature changes during a piece of music, you will usually see a thin double bar line at the **key change**. You may also see natural signs reminding you to "cancel" previous sharps or flats. Keep playing, using the correct notes indicated in the *new* key signature.

28. MOLLY MALONE

Irish Folk Song

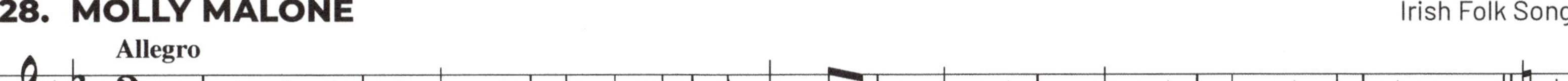

Dynamics

cresc. = crescendo (or)
decresc. = decrescendo (or)

29. RISE AND FALL

30. NO COMPARISON

31. SIGHTREADING CHALLENGE

Remember the S-T-A-R-S guidelines.

THEORY
¢ Time Signature
Cut Time (Alla Breve)
or
= 2 beats per measure
= Half note gets one beat
= 2 beats
= 1 beat
= ½ beat
32. RHYTHM RAP Clap the rhythm while counting and tapping.
Clap
1 & 2 &
33. A CUT ABOVE
34. TWO-FOUR YANKEE DOODLE
American Folk Song
Moderato
mf
35. CUT TIME YANKEE DOODLE
American Folk Song
Moderato
mf
36. MARIANNE
Jamaican Folk Song
Moderato
Rolls Xylo. only
p cresc.
f decresc.
p
37. THE VICTORS
Louis Elbel
March Tempo
f
Count ► 1 & 2 &
Rolls Xylo. only
38. ESSENTIAL CREATIVITY Write this example in cut time ¢ before playing.
Allegro
f
Allegro

Dynamics

mp – *mezzo piano* (moderately soft)   *p* – *mp* – *mf* – *f*

39. A - ROVING

Syncopation

Syncopation occurs when an accent or emphasis is given to a note that is not on a strong beat. This type of "off-beat" feel is common in many popular and classical styles.

THEORY

40. RHYTHM RAP

41. IN SYNC

42. LA ROCA

Puerto Rican Folk Song

American composer **George M. Cohan** (1878–1942) was also a popular author, producer, director and performer. He helped develop a popular form of American musical theater now known as musical comedy. He is also considered to be one of the most famous composers of American patriotic songs, earning the Congressional Medal of Honor in 1917 for his song *Over There*. Many of his songs became morale boosters when the United States entered World War I in that same year.

HISTORY

43. ESSENTIAL ELEMENTS QUIZ – YOU'RE A GRAND OLD FLAG

Words and Music by George M. Cohan

THEORY

New Key Signature

This key signature indicates your **Key of C** (no flats or sharps).

44. KEY MOMENT – New Note

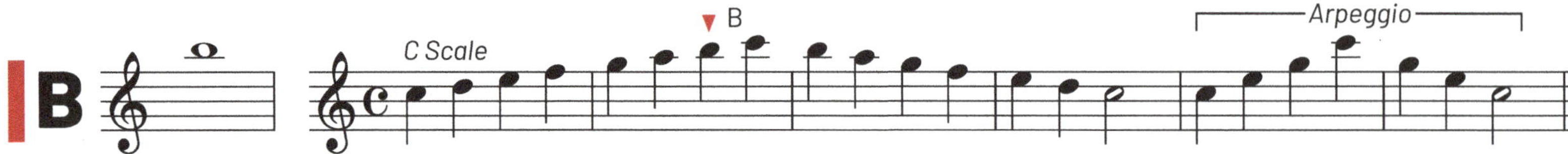

45. THE MINSTREL BOY

Irish Folk Song

46. CLOSE CALL – New Note

47. VICTORY MARCH

M. J. Shea

THEORY

Cut Time Syncopation

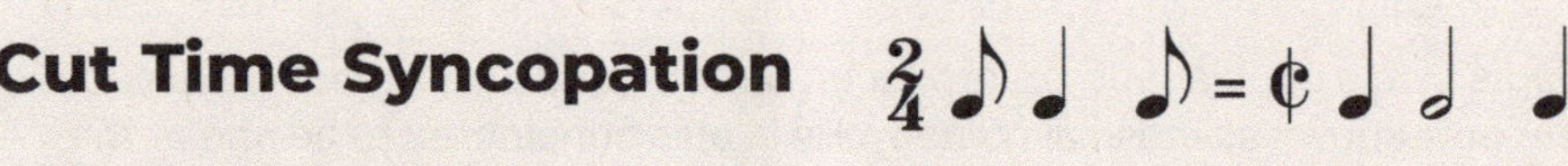

Compare the notation of the melody below with *Victory March* above. Should they sound the same?

48. WINNING STREAK

M. J. Shea

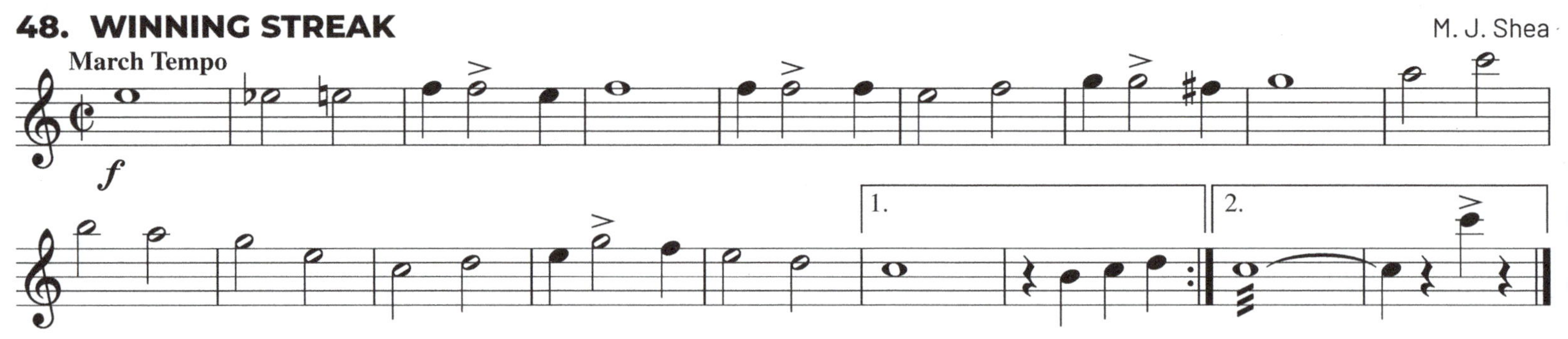

49. SIGHTREADING CHALLENGE *Remember the S-T-A-R-S guidelines.*

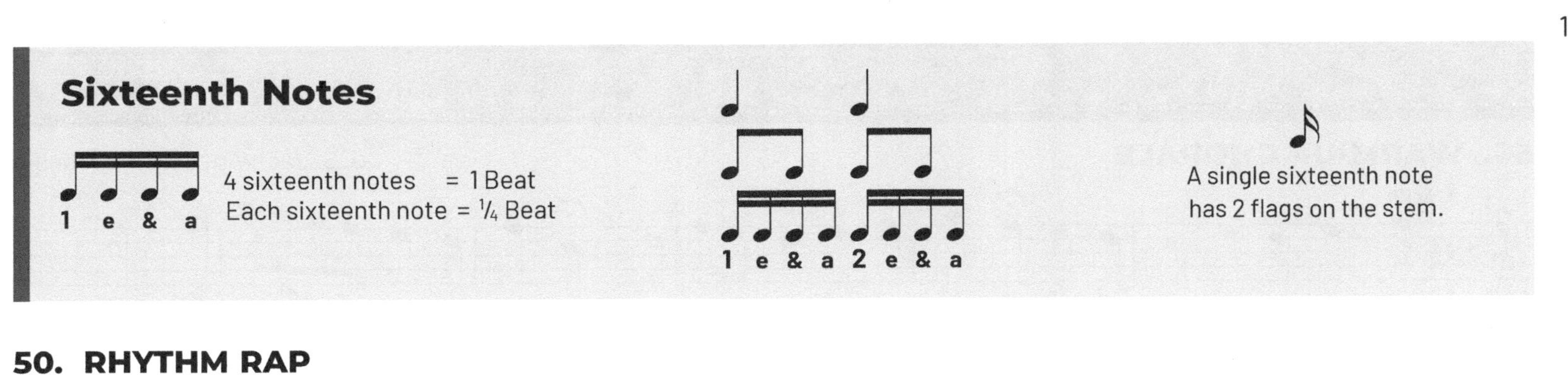

50. RHYTHM RAP

51. SIXTEENTH NOTE FANFARE

52. MOVING ALONG

53. BACK AND FORTH – Duet

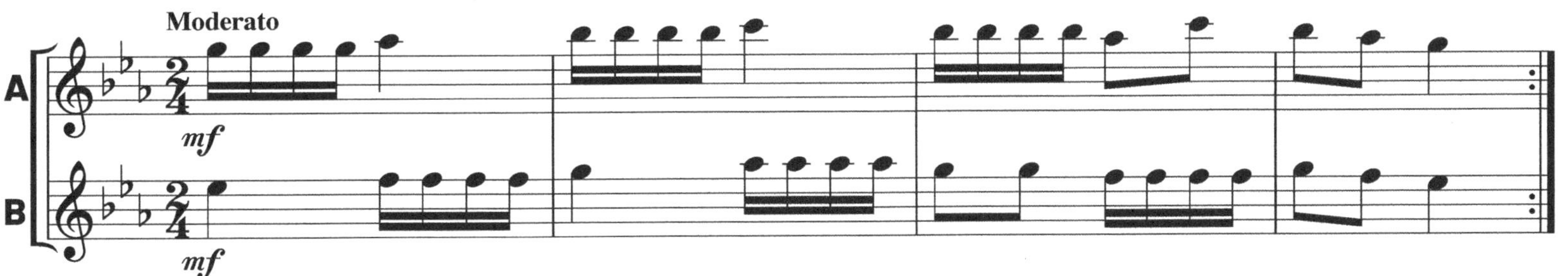

54. COMIN' ROUND THE MOUNTAIN VARIATIONS

American Folk Song

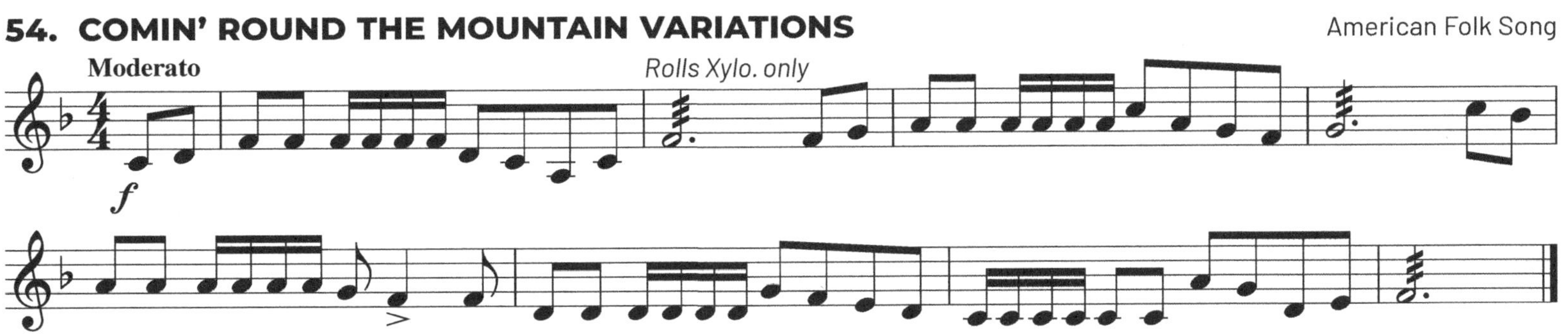

55. ESSENTIAL ELEMENTS QUIZ

PERFORMANCE SPOTLIGHT
56. WARM-UP CHORALE
J. S. Bach/Arr. by John Higgins
Largo
p
mp
p
rit.
57. THE THUNDERER – Band Arrangement
John Philip Sousa
Arr. by John Higgins
March style
mf cresc.
f
5
13
Fine
mf
D.C. al Fine
Reproduced by Permission of Boosey & Hawkes Music Publishers Ltd.
58. HILL AND GULLY RIDER – Band Arrangement
Jamaican Folk Song
Arr. by John Higgins
Moderato
2
3
f
7
mf
11
f
1.
2.
p
f
59. SHENANDOAH – Band Arrangement
American Folk Song
Arr. by John Higgins
Largo
p
5
mf
11
p
rit.

PERFORMANCE SPOTLIGHT

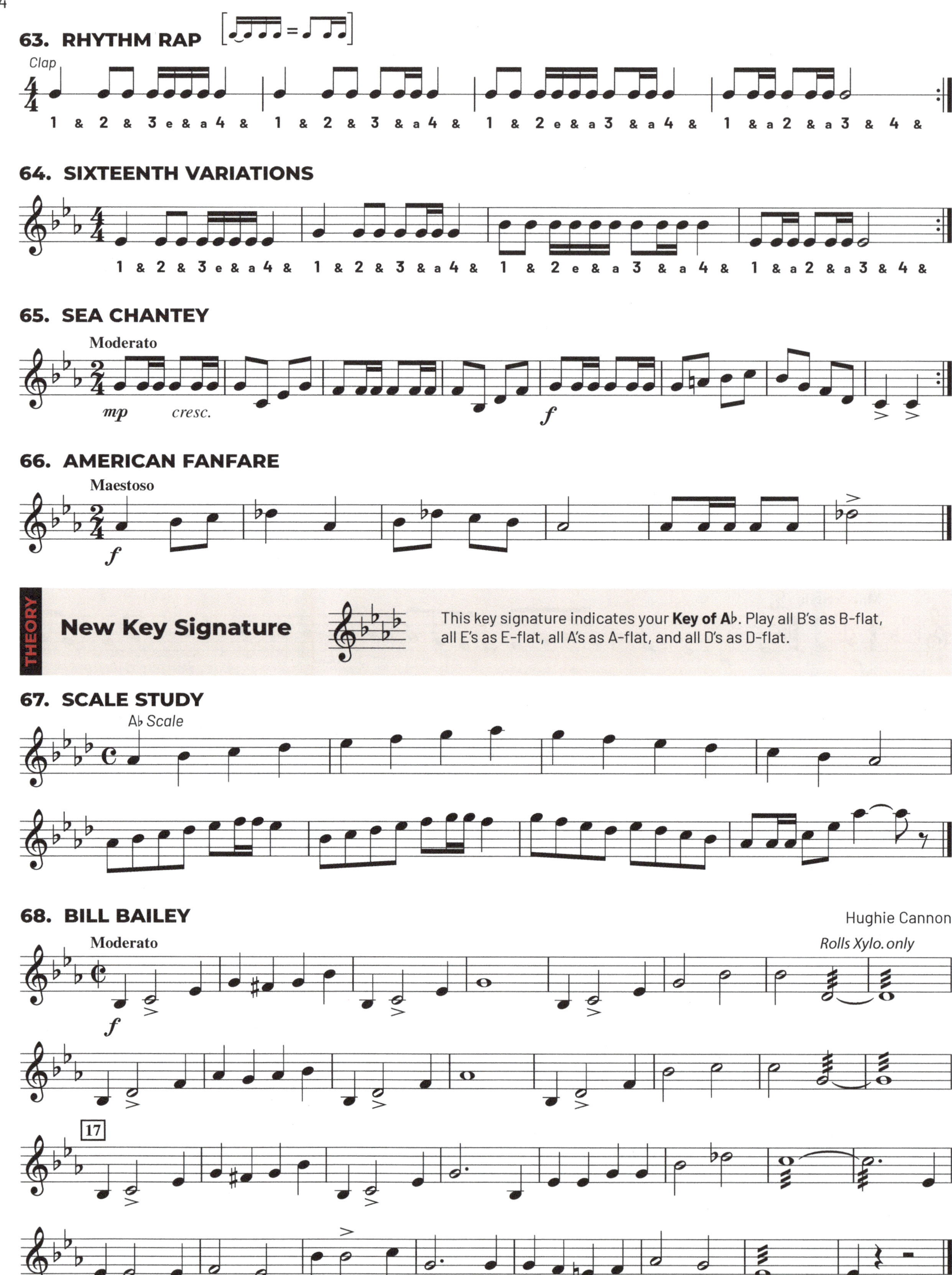
63. RHYTHM RAP
Clap
1 & 2 & 3 e & a 4 & 1 & 2 & 3 & a 4 & 1 & 2 e & a 3 & a 4 & 1 & a 2 & a 3 & 4 &
64. SIXTEENTH VARIATIONS
1 & 2 & 3 e & a 4 & 1 & 2 & 3 & a 4 & 1 & 2 e & a 3 & a 4 & 1 & a 2 & a 3 & 4 &
65. SEA CHANTEY
Moderato
mp
cresc.
f
66. AMERICAN FANFARE
Maestoso
f
THEORY
New Key Signature
This key signature indicates your Key of A♭. Play all B's as B-flat, all E's as E-flat, all A's as A-flat, and all D's as D-flat.
67. SCALE STUDY
A♭ Scale
68. BILL BAILEY
Hughie Cannon
Moderato
Rolls Xylo. only
f
17

69. RHYTHM RAP

70. RHYTHM ETUDE

71. BATTLE STATIONS

72. ENGLISH DANCE

73. BIG ROCK CANDY MOUNTAIN

American Folk Song

74. ESSENTIAL ELEMENTS QUIZ

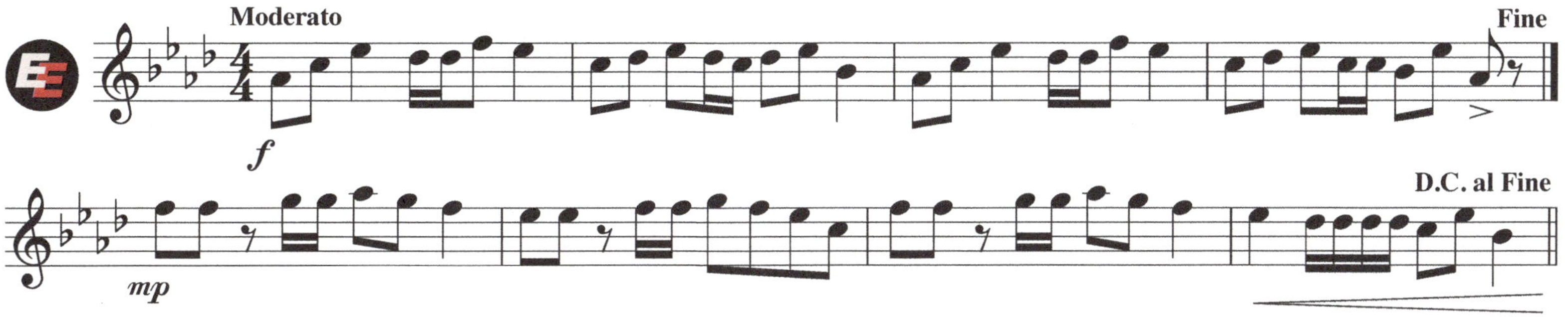

Looking for some more fun music to play?
See the inside front cover for instructions on accessing recent popular Bonus Songs.

Rallentando *rall.* - Gradually slower (same as *ritardando*).

75. SIMPLE SONG – Duet

76. LINE DANCE

77. TECHNIQUE TRAX

78. THE GALWAY PIPER

Irish Reel

79. MANHATTAN BEACH MARCH

John Philip Sousa

80. SIGHTREADING CHALLENGE *Remember the S-T-A-R-S guidelines.*

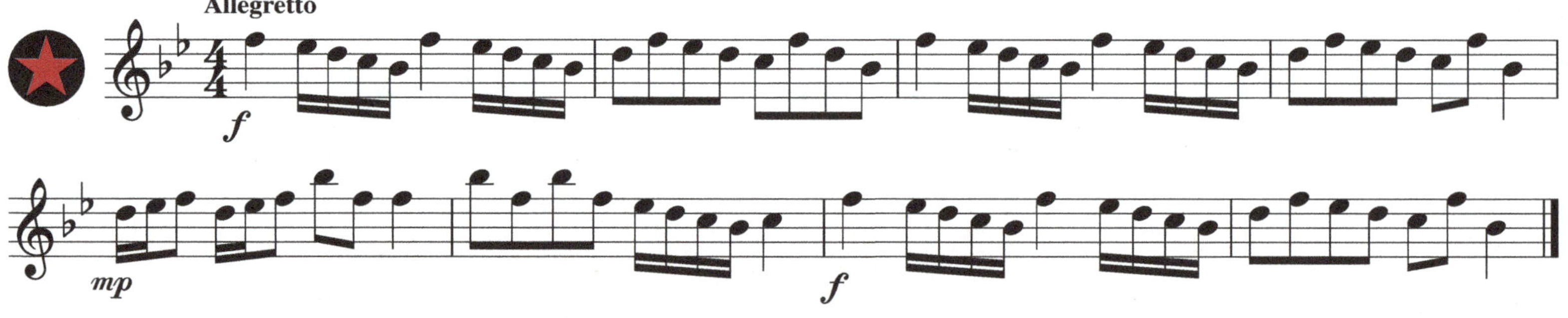

81. RHYTHM RAP
Clap
1 e & a 2 & 3 & a 4 & 1 & a 2 & 3 & a 4 & 1 & a 2 & 3 & a 4 & 1 & a 2 & 3 & 4 &
82. MARCHING ALONG
1 e & a 2 & 3 & a 4 & 1 & a 2 & 3 & a 4 & 1 & a 2 & 3 & a 4 & 1 & a 2 & 3 & 4 &
83. FANFARE FOR BAND – Trio
Roll Xylo. only
Maestoso
A
B
C
f
84. O TANNENBAUM
German Carol
Andante
mp
1.
2.
mf
f
rall.
85. S'VIVON
Traditional Hanukkah Song
Moderato
mf
f
mp
86. GOOD KING WENCESLAS
English Carol
Allegretto
mf
rit.

DAILY WARM-UPS

WORK-OUTS FOR TONE & TECHNIQUE

87. TONE BUILDER *Play at a very slow tempo.*

88. FLEXIBILITY STUDY

89. TECHNIQUE TRAX

90. CHORALE

Johann Sebastian Bach

Adagio

p *mp* *p*

mf *mp* *rall.* *p*

HISTORY

French composer **Georges Bizet** (1838–1875) entered the Paris Conservatory to study music when he was only ten years old. There he won many awards for voice, piano, organ, and composition. Bizet's best known composition is the opera *Carmen*, which was first performed in 1875. *Carmen* tells the story of a band of Gypsies, soldiers, smugglers, and outlaws. Originally criticized for its realism on stage, it was soon hailed as the most popular French opera ever written.

91. TOREADOR SONG (from CARMEN)

Georges Bizet

92. LA CUMPARSITA – New Note (Enharmonic)

G. Rodriguez

93. THE YELLOW ROSE OF TEXAS *Check the key signature.*

American Folk Song

94. SCALE STUDY

Until 1974 Australia's official national anthem was *God Save The Queen*. A competition was held in 1973 to compose a new anthem, but none of the entries met with the judges' approval. Finally the government asked the public to vote, choosing from among Australia's 3 most popular patriotic songs. After easily defeating *Waltzing Matilda* and *God Save The Queen*, *Advance Australia Fair* was officially declared the national anthem of Australia on April 19, 1974.

HISTORY

95. ADVANCE AUSTRALIA FAIR

Peter Dodds McCormick

96. ESSENTIAL CREATIVITY

Arrange the melody of "America (My Country 'Tis Of Thee)" for your instrument. Write out the first line (6 measures). Your first note is F. ADD: Key signature—key of F • Time signature—3/4 • Tempo and dynamic markings.

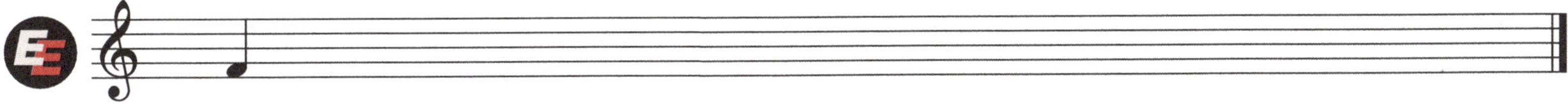

Play the completed line on your instrument to hear your own version.

97. AMERICAN PATROL

F. W. Meacham

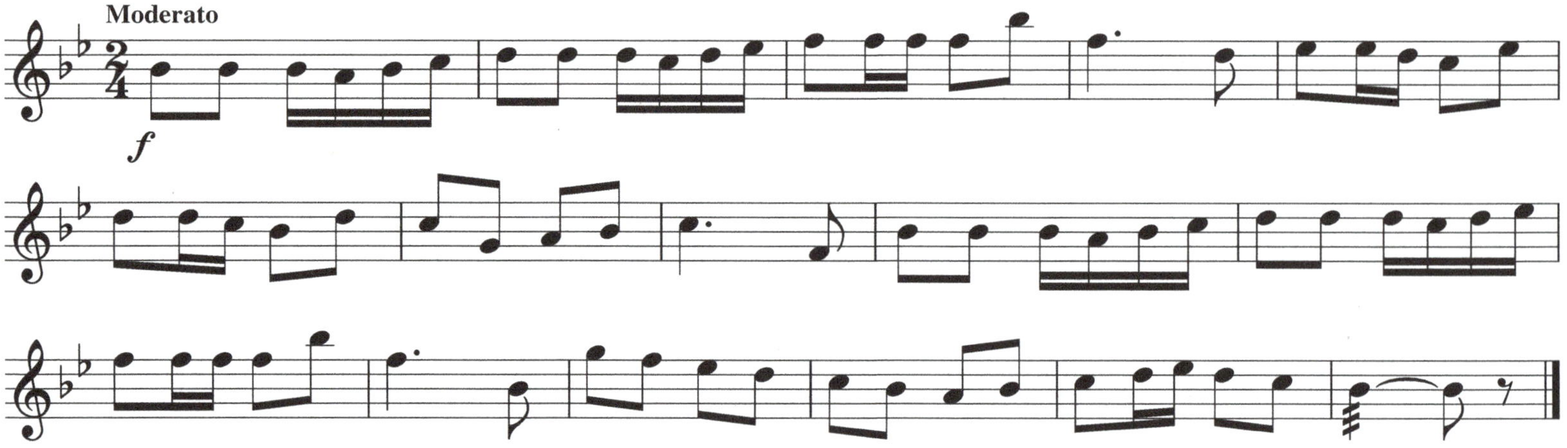
Moderato
f

98. ARIA (from MARRIAGE OF FIGARO)

Wolfgang Amadeus Mozart

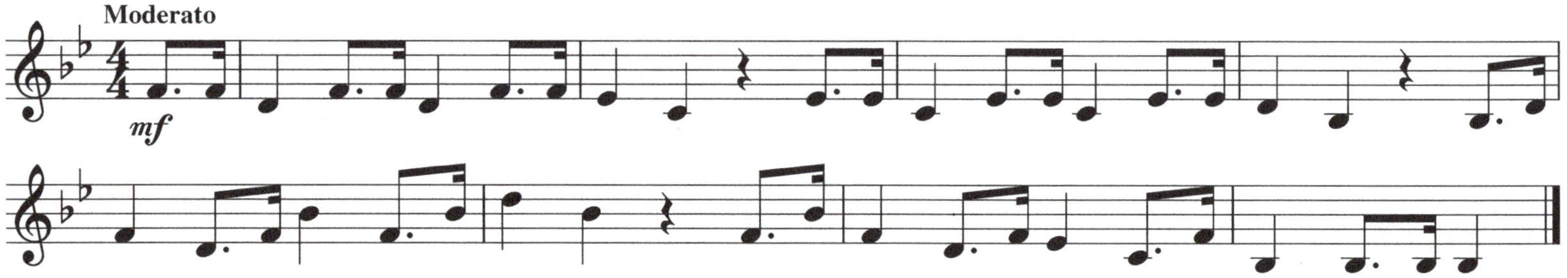
Moderato
mf

HISTORY

American composer **John Philip Sousa** (1854-1932) was best known for his brilliant band marches. Sousa wrote 136 marches, including *The Stars and Stripes Forever*, which was declared the official march of the United States of America in 1987.

99. THE STARS AND STRIPES FOREVER

John Philip Sousa

March Tempo
f
Rolls Xylo. only
Check rhythm
17

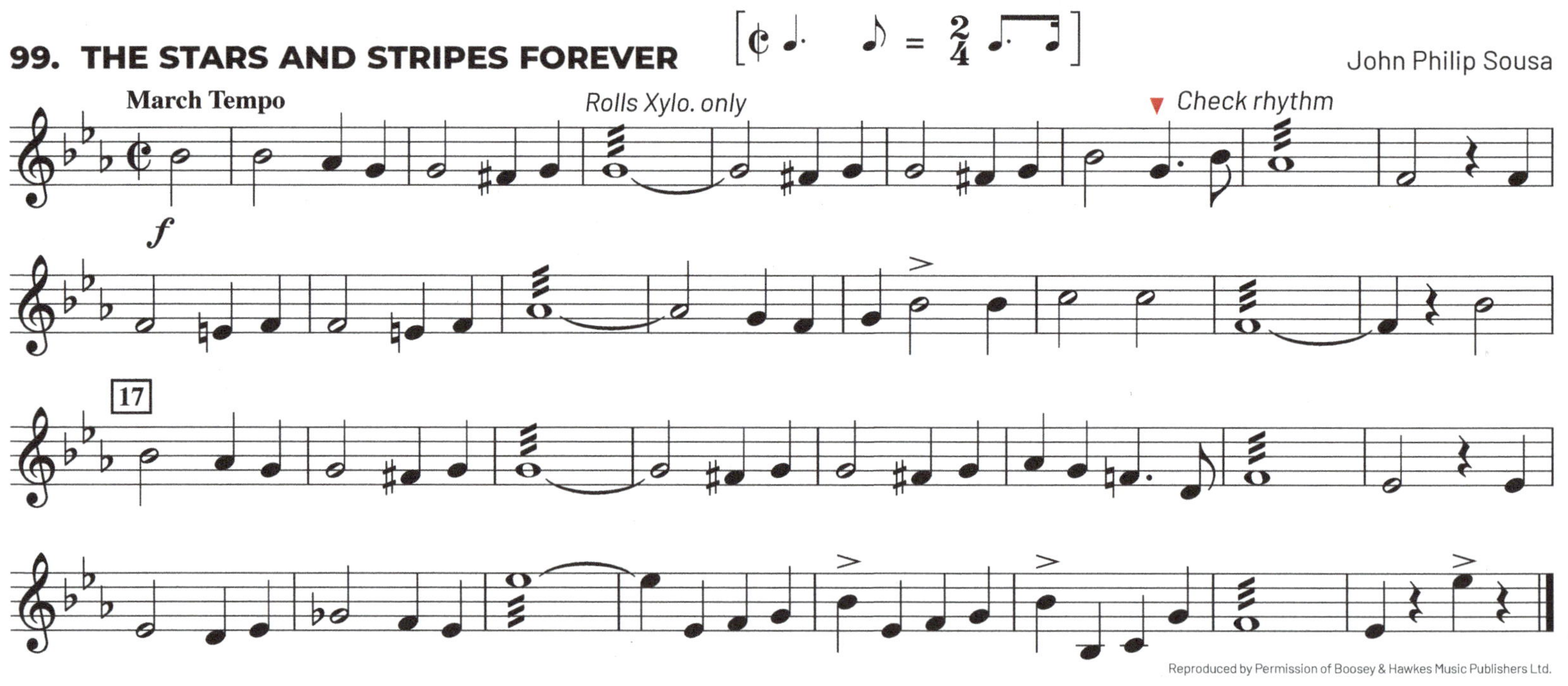

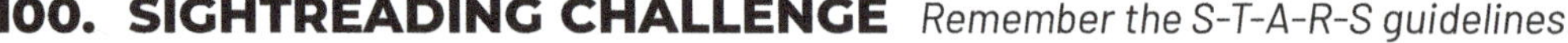

100. SIGHTREADING CHALLENGE *Remember the S-T-A-R-S guidelines.*

Moderato
mf
f

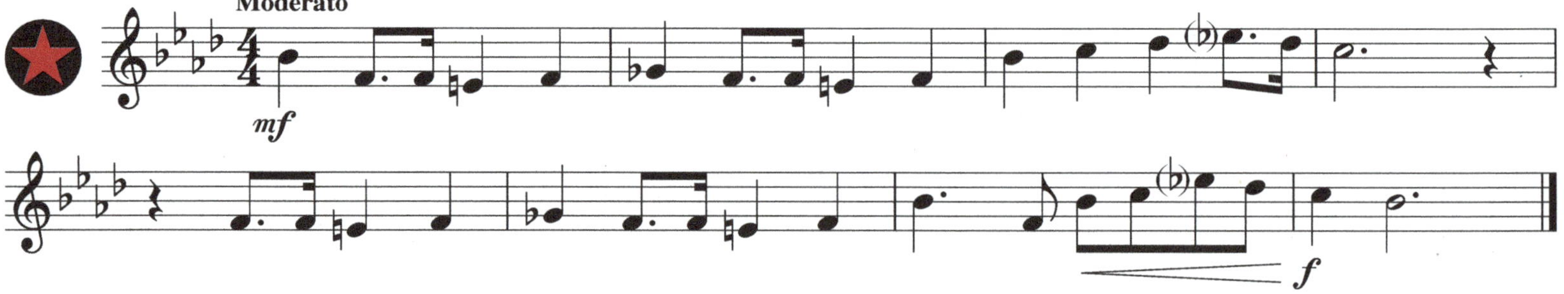

$\frac{6}{8}$ Time Signature

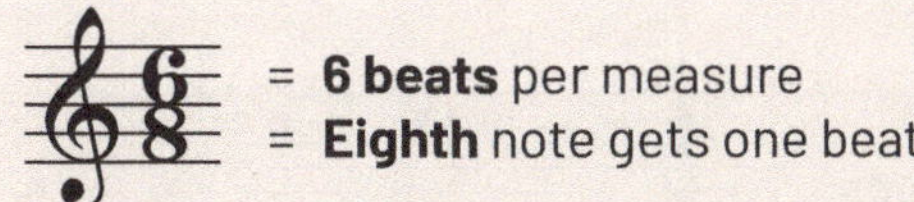

= **6 beats** per measure
= **Eighth** note gets one beat

♪ = 1 beat ♩ = 2 beats
♩. = 3 beats 𝅗𝅥. = 6 beats

6/8 time is usually played with a slight emphasis on the **1st** and **4th** beats of each measure. This divides the measure into 2 groups of 3 beats each. In faster music, these two primary beats will make the music feel like it's counted "in 2."

THEORY

101. RHYTHM RAP *Clap the rhythm while counting and tapping.*

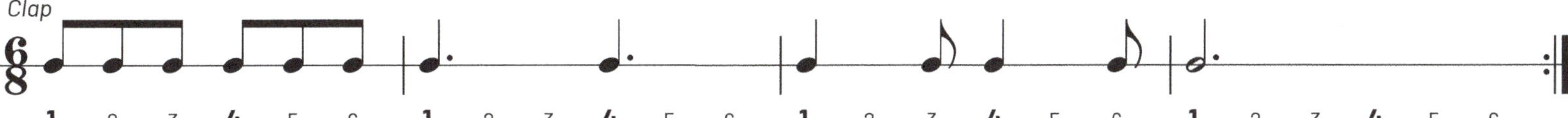

102. LAZY DAY

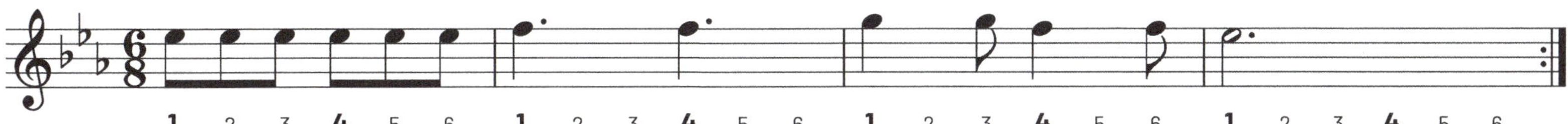

103. ROW YOUR BOAT

104. JOLLY GOOD FELLOW

105. CHANSON

French Folk Song

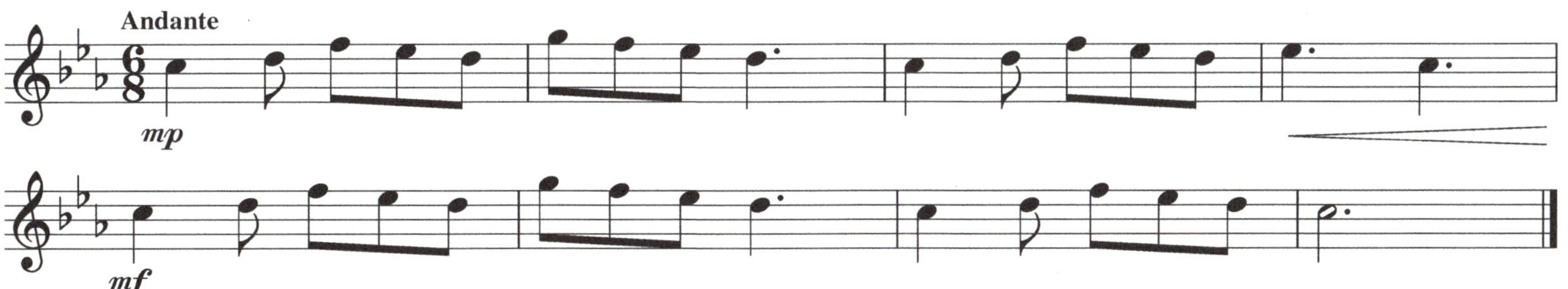

106. ESSENTIAL ELEMENTS QUIZ – WHEN JOHNNY COMES MARCHING HOME

American Folk Song

THEORY

More Enharmonics

Remember that notes which sound the same but have different letter names are called **enharmonics**. These are some common enharmonics that you'll use in the exercises below.

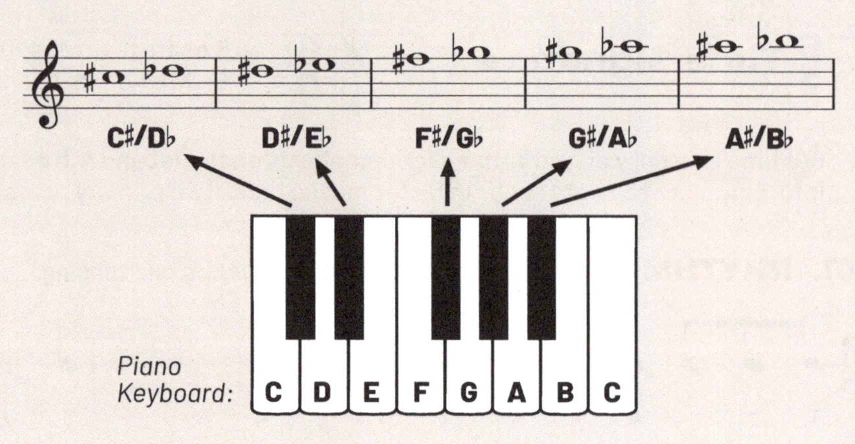

More Chromatics

The smallest distance between two notes is a half-step, and a scale made up of consecutive half-steps is a **chromatic scale**. These are usually written with **enharmonic** notes—sharps when going up and flats when going down.

107. CHROMATIC SCALE

Practice slowly until you are sure of all the notes.

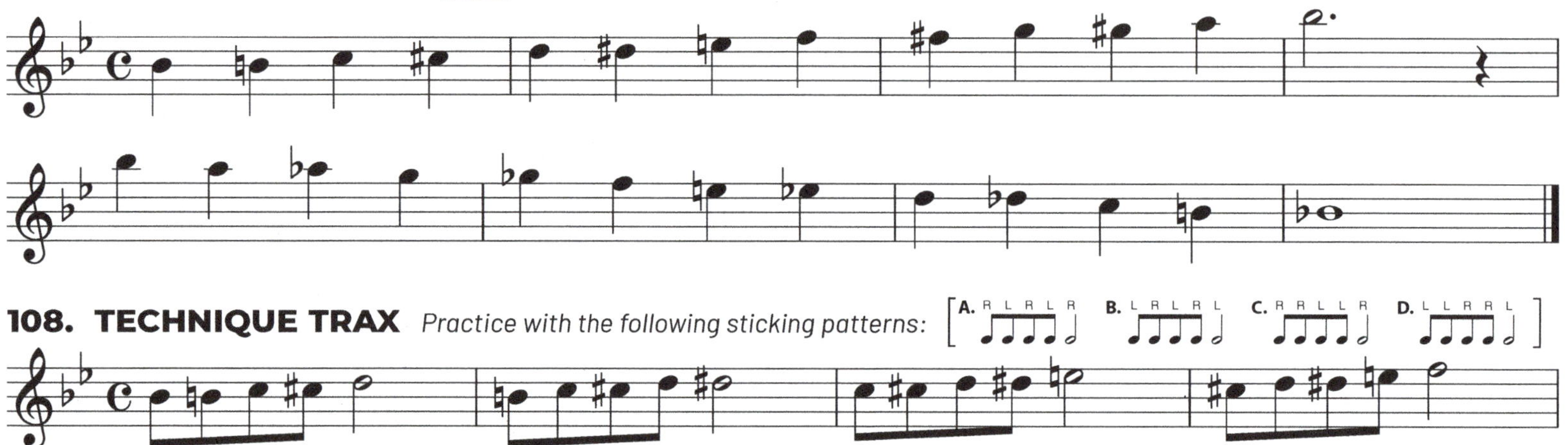

108. TECHNIQUE TRAX

Practice with the following sticking patterns: A. R L R L R B. L R L R L C. R R L L R D. L L R R L

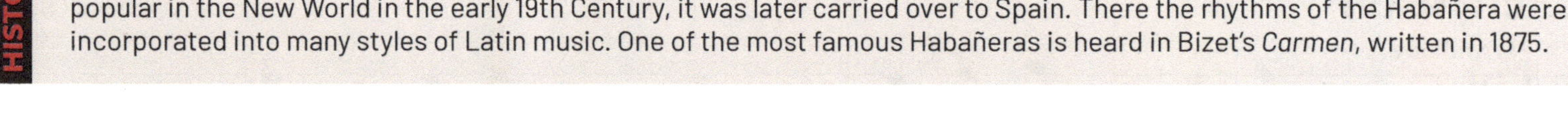

HISTORY

A **Habañera** is a Cuban dance and song form in slow 2/4 meter. It is named after the city of Havana, the capital of Cuba. Made popular in the New World in the early 19th Century, it was later carried over to Spain. There the rhythms of the Habañera were incorporated into many styles of Latin music. One of the most famous Habañeras is heard in Bizet's *Carmen*, written in 1875.

109. HABAÑERA (from CARMEN)

Georges Bizet

110. CHROMATIC CRESCENDO

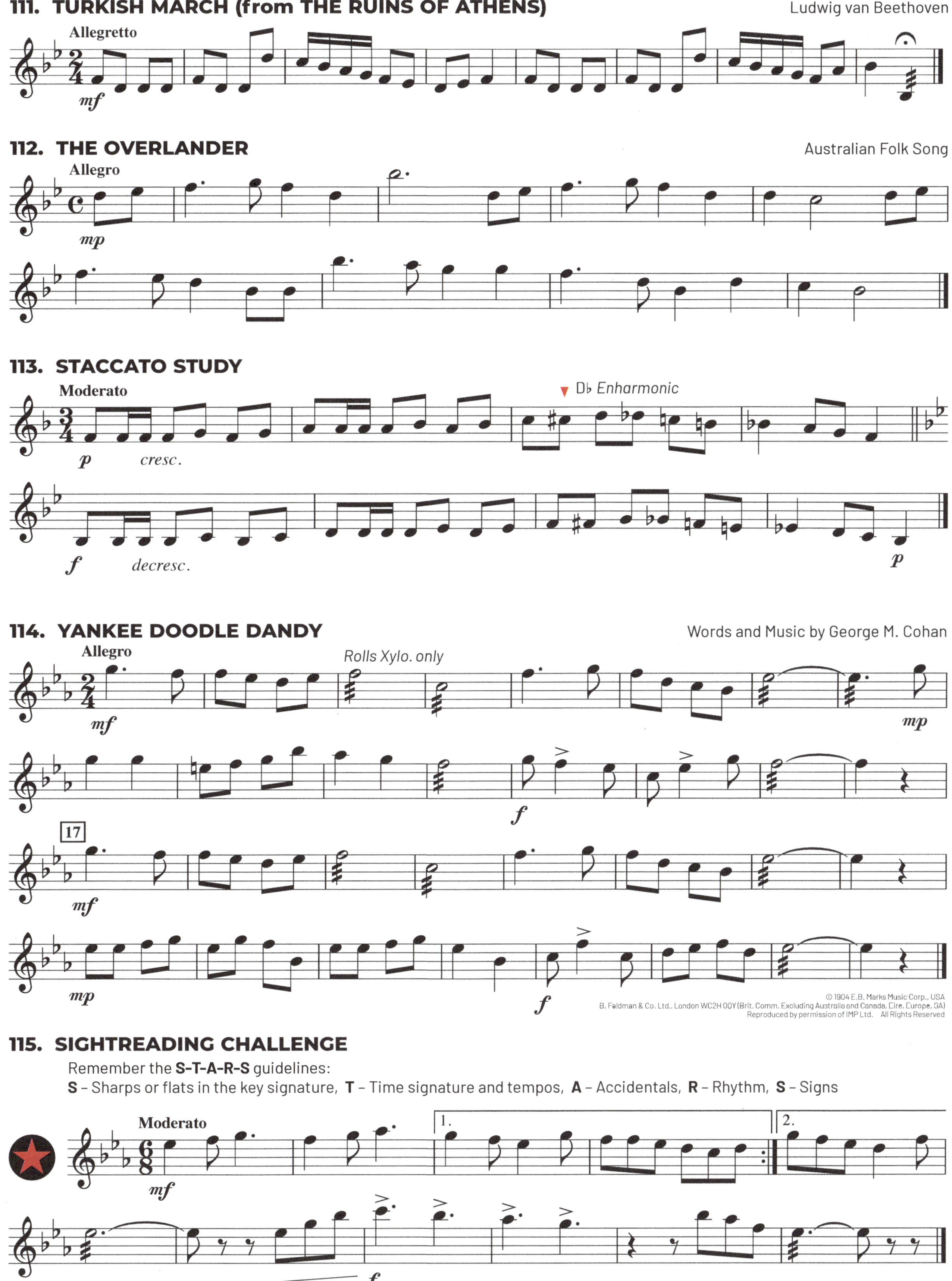
111. TURKISH MARCH (from THE RUINS OF ATHENS)
Ludwig van Beethoven
Allegretto
mf
112. THE OVERLANDER
Australian Folk Song
Allegro
mp
113. STACCATO STUDY
Moderato
p
cresc.
D♭ Enharmonic
f
decresc.
p
114. YANKEE DOODLE DANDY
Words and Music by George M. Cohan
Allegro
mf
Rolls Xylo. only
mp
f
17
mf
mp
f
© 1904 E.B. Marks Music Corp., USA
B. Feldman & Co. Ltd., London WC2H 0QY (Brit. Comm. Excluding Australia and Canada, Eire, Europe, SA)
Reproduced by permission of IMP Ltd. All Rights Reserved
115. SIGHTREADING CHALLENGE
Remember the S-T-A-R-S guidelines:
S - Sharps or flats in the key signature, T - Time signature and tempos, A - Accidentals, R - Rhythm, S - Signs
Moderato
mf
1.
2.
f

Triplets

A **triplet** is a group of **3** notes played in the space of **2**. In $\frac{2}{4}$, $\frac{3}{4}$, or $\frac{4}{4}$ time, an eighth note triplet is spread evenly across one beat.

116. RHYTHM RAP

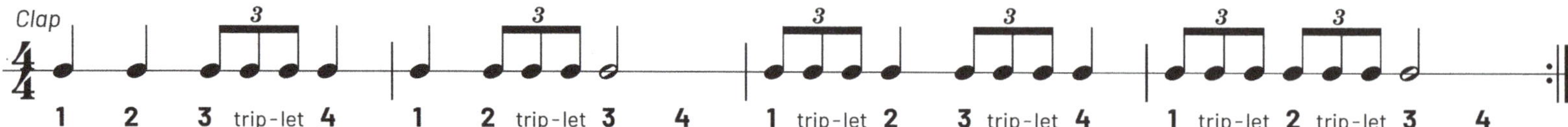

117. THREE TO GET READY

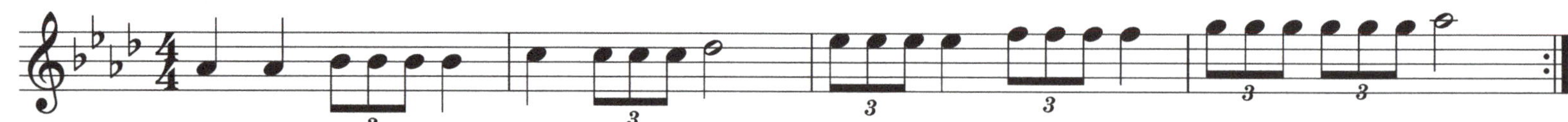

118. TRIPLET STUDY

119. MARCH (from THE NUTCRACKER) – Duet

Peter I. Tchaikovsky

120. ESSENTIAL ELEMENTS QUIZ – THEME FROM FAUST

Charles Gounod

121. SCALE STUDY
F Scale
3
Check Rhythm
122. OVER THE RIVER AND THROUGH THE WOODS
American Folk Song
Allegretto
mf
f
1.
decresc.
2.
123. RHYTHM RAP
Clap
1 & 2 e & a 3 & 4 &
1 & 2 & a 3 & 4 &
1 & 2 & a 3 & 4 &
1 & 2 & a 3 & 4 &
124. ON THE MOVE
125. HIGHER GROUND
Moderato
mf
3
f
126. ESSENTIAL ELEMENTS QUIZ
Allegretto
mf
9
p
mf

HISTORY The first known printing of the lyrics and music to **The Marines' Hymn** dates from August 1, 1918. An unknown author is believed to have taken the opening words of the song from the words on the Marine Corps flag, "From the halls of Montezuma to the shores of Tripoli." The music was taken from "Genevieve de Brabant," by the operetta composer Jacques Offenbach.

127. THE MARINES' HYMN

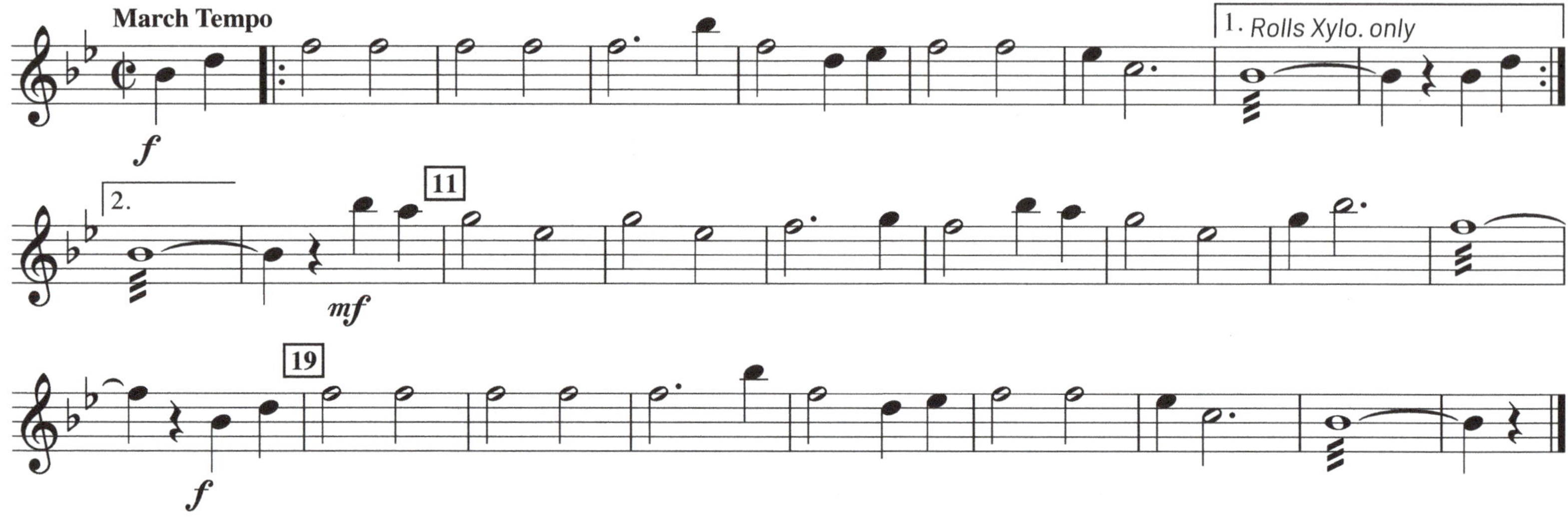

D.S. al Fine

Play until you see the **D.S. al Fine**. Then go back to the sign (𝄋) and play until the word **Fine**. **D.S.** is the abbreviation for **Dal Segno**, or "from the sign," and **Fine** means "the end."

128. D.S. MARCH

Accelerando

accel. – Gradually faster.

129. CAN-CAN

Jacques Offenbach

130. TARANTELLA

Italian Folk Song

The **waltz** is a dance in moderate 3/4 time which developed around 1800 from the Ländler, an Austrian peasant dance. Austrian composer **Johann Strauss, Jr.** (1825–1899) composed over 400 waltzes. These include such famous pieces as *The Blue Danube*, *Tales From the Vienna Woods* and *Emperor Waltz*.

HISTORY

131. EMPEROR WALTZ

Johann Strauss, Jr.

Legato Style

legato – Played in a smooth, connected style.

Use a slow up-stroke when playing legato style.

132. ENGLISH DANCE – Duet

Johann Christian Bach

133. ESSENTIAL ELEMENTS QUIZ – BRITISH GRENADIERS

Traditional

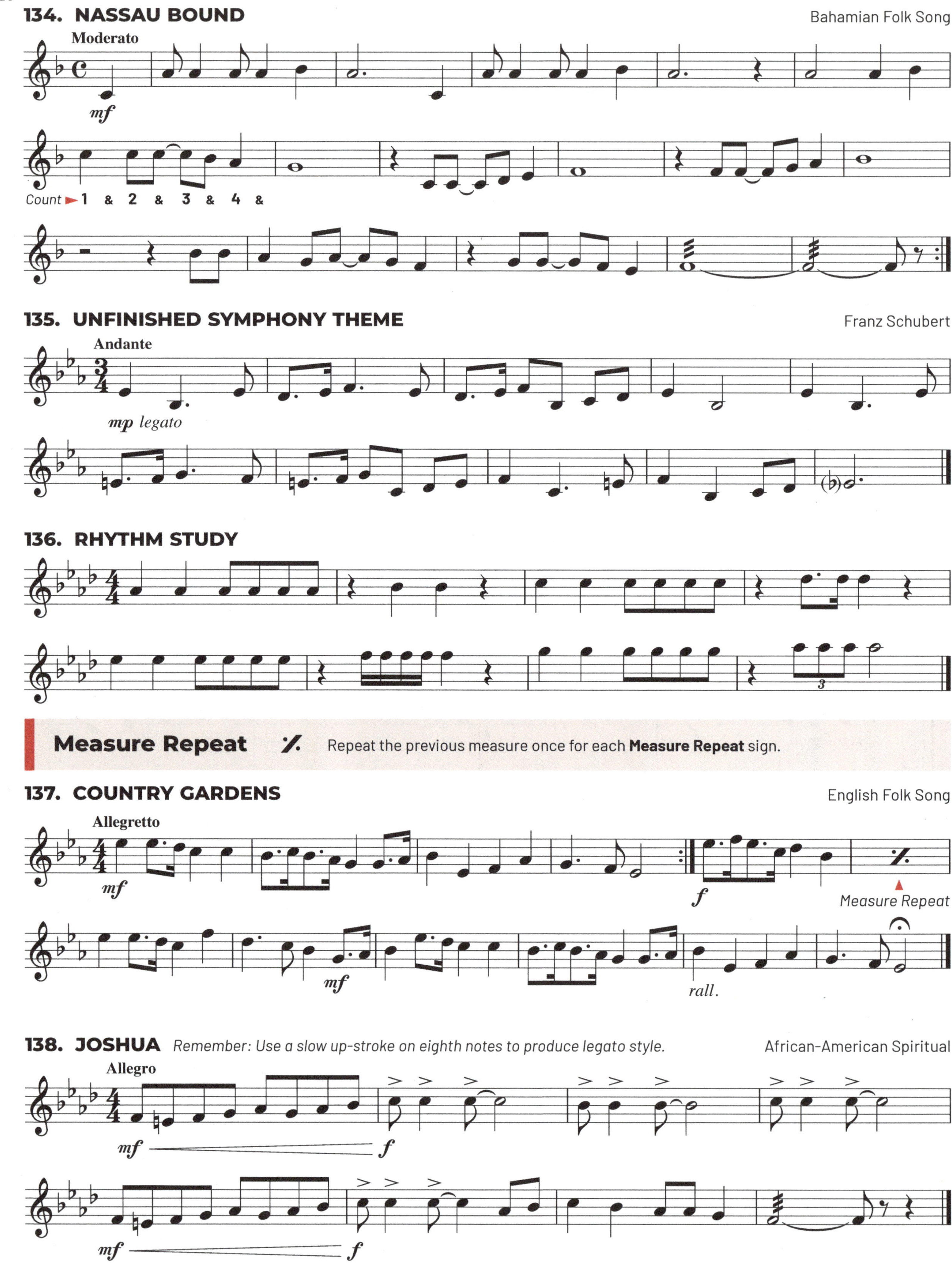
134. NASSAU BOUND
Bahamian Folk Song
Moderato
mf
Count ► 1 & 2 & 3 & 4 &
135. UNFINISHED SYMPHONY THEME
Franz Schubert
Andante
mp legato
136. RHYTHM STUDY
3
Measure Repeat
Repeat the previous measure once for each Measure Repeat sign.
137. COUNTRY GARDENS
English Folk Song
Allegretto
mf
f
Measure Repeat
mf
rall.
138. JOSHUA
Remember: Use a slow up-stroke on eighth notes to produce legato style.
African-American Spiritual
Allegro
mf
f
mf
f

139. LISTEN TO THE MOCKINGBIRD

Alice Hawthorne

Moderato

mf ▶ Pick-up

140. ANCHORS AWEIGH

Capt. A.H. Miles and C.A. Zimmerman

March Tempo

f *mf* *cresc.*

1. 2.

f *f*

141. GREENSLEEVES

Remember: Use a slow up-stroke on eighth notes to produce legato style.

English Folk Song

Andante

p *mf*

rit.

142. THE LONG CLIMB

▲ *Measure Repeat*

143. THE BLUE BELLS OF SCOTLAND

Scottish Folk Song

Moderato

1. 2.

f *mf*

f

THEORY

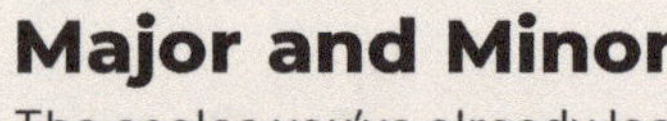

Major and Minor

The scales you've already learned are called **Major** scales. They all follow the same pattern, with **half-steps** between notes 3–4 and between notes 7–8.

Natural Minor scales follow a different pattern, with **half-steps** between notes 2–3 and 5–6. The **G Minor** scale uses the same key signature as **B♭ Major**.

Another type of minor scale is called **Harmonic Minor**, which adds an accidental to raise the **7th** note by a half-step. Compare the scales on the right.

See page 37 for additional minor scales.

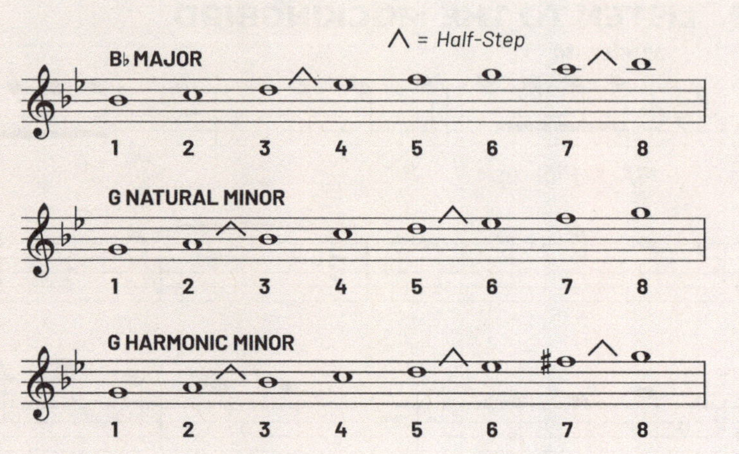

144. NATURAL MINOR SCALE

145. FINALE FROM "NEW WORLD SYMPHONY"

Antonin Dvorák

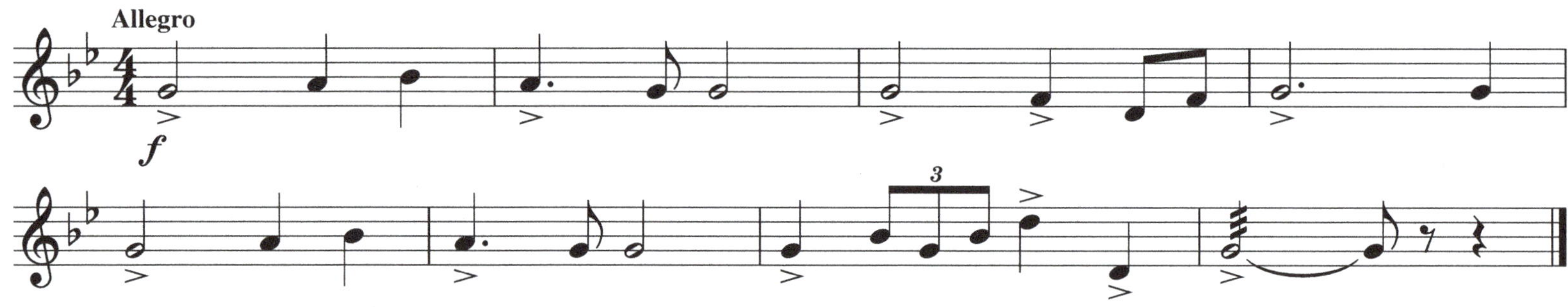

146. HARMONIC MINOR SCALE

147. HUNGARIAN DANCE NO. 5

Johannes Brahms

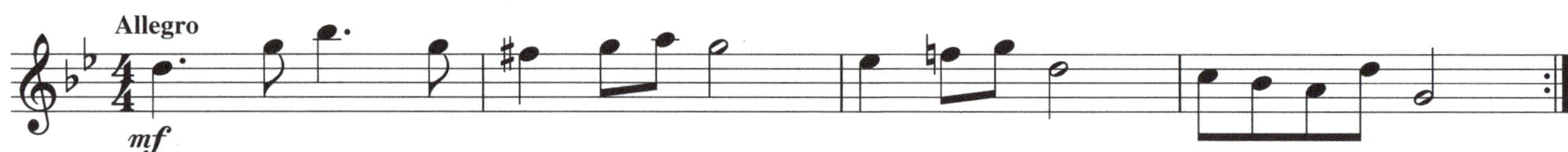

148. POMP AND CIRCUMSTANCE (LAND OF HOPE AND GLORY)

Edward Elgar

PERFORMANCE SPOTLIGHT

D.S. al Coda Play until you see the **D.S. al Coda**. Then go back to the sign (𝄋) and play until the **Coda Sign** ("To Coda" ⊕). Skip directly to the **Coda** and play until the end.

149. SIMPLE GIFTS – Band Arrangement

Shaker Folk Song
Arr. by John Higgins

150. SEMPER FIDELIS – Band Arrangement

John Philip Sousa
Arr. by John Higgins

PERFORMANCE SPOTLIGHT

151. DANNY BOY – Band Arrangement

Irish Folk Song
Arr. by John Higgins

152. TAKE ME OUT TO THE BALL GAME – Band Arrangement

By Jack Norworth and Harry von Tilzer
Arr. by John Higgins

Additional Bonus Songs are available online. See the inside front cover for details.

PERFORMANCE SPOTLIGHT

153. SERENGETI (AFRICAN RHAPSODY) – Band Arrangement

John Higgins

RUBANK® STUDIES

RUBANK® STUDIES

KEY OF E♭

163.

164.

165.

166.

KEY OF F

167.

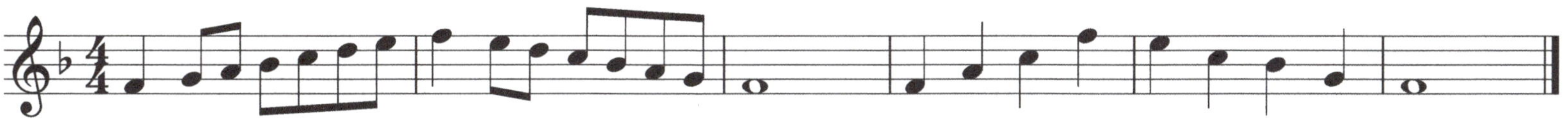

168.

169.

170.

RUBANK® STUDIES

KEY OF A♭

171.

172.

173.

174.

KEY OF C

175.

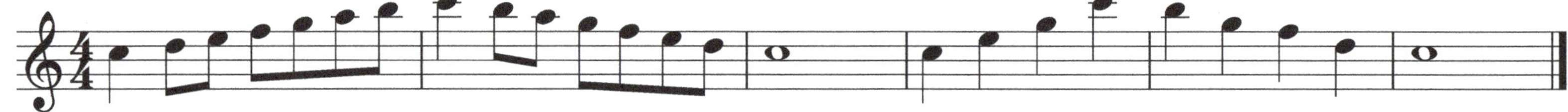

176.

177.

178.

RUBANK® STUDIES

INDIVIDUAL STUDY – Keyboard Percussion

187. C MAJOR SCALE STUDY

188. ARPEGGIO STUDY

189. SEQUENCE STUDY

190. DOUBLE STICKING ETUDE

191. OCTAVE ARPEGGIO ETUDE

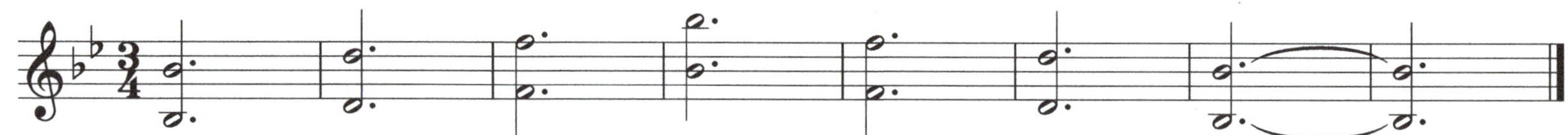

192. OCTAVE SCALE ETUDE

193. CHROMATIC SCALE CHALLENGE

INDIVIDUAL STUDY – Keyboard Percussion

INDIVIDUAL STUDY – Keyboard Percussion

Solo with Piano Accompaniment

You can perform this solo with the piano accompaniment on the following page.

200. INTERMEZZO from "Carmen" – Orchestra Bells Solo

Online audio – see inside front cover to access.

Georges Bizet
Arr. by Will Rapp

INDIVIDUAL STUDY – Keyboard Percussion

200. INTERMEZZO from "Carmen" – Piano Accompaniment

Online audio – see inside front cover to access.

Georges Bizet
Arr. by Will Rapp

INDIVIDUAL STUDY – Keyboard Percussion

Solo with Piano Accompaniment

You can perform this solo with the piano accompaniment on the following page.

201. GYPSY DANCE from "Carmen" – Xylophone Solo

Georges Bizet
Arr. by Will Rapp

Online audio - see inside front cover to access.

INDIVIDUAL STUDY – Keyboard Percussion

201. GYPSY DANCE from "Carmen" – Piano Accompaniment

Georges Bizet
Arr. by Will Rapp

Online audio – see inside front cover to access.

RHYTHM STUDIES

RHYTHM STUDIES

CREATING MUSIC

THEORY

Theme and Variation

Theme and Variation is a technique used by composers and arrangers to create interesting musical ideas that are "varied" from an established melody, or "theme." Play the following theme and two variations to hear how the arranger has created new phrases based on the original melody.

1. THEME

"Simple Gifts"

2. THEME AND YOUR VARIATION

Write your own variation of this theme. Use your instrument to hear and try different ideas.

"Candy Mountain Rock"

Theme

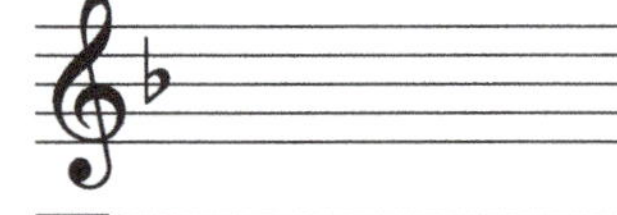

THEORY

Blues Improvisation

Improvisation using a **Blues Scale** is an important part of jazz and popular music. Musicians use combinations of these notes and various rhythms to create their own spontaneous solos over a 12 measure progression of chords.

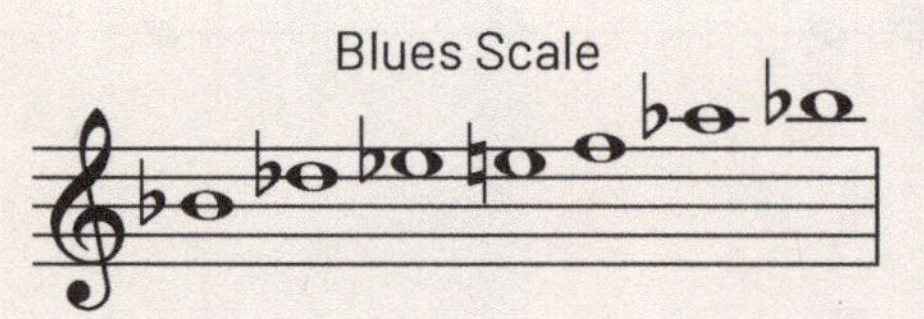

3. LET'S JAM

Use the indicated notes from the Blues Scale to create your own solo to play with the accompaniment (Line B).

You can mark your progress through the book on this page.
Fill in the stars as instructed by your band director.

1. Page 2–4, Review
2. Page 5, Sightreading Challenge, No. 19
3. Page 6, Daily Warm-Ups
4. Page 7, Sightreading Challenge, No. 31
5. Page 8, Essential Creativity, No. 38
6. Page 9, EE Quiz, No. 43
7. Page 10, Sightreading Challenge, No. 49
8. Page 11, EE Quiz, No. 55
9. Page 12–13, Performance Spotlight
10. Page 15, EE Quiz, No. 74
11. Page 16, Sightreading Challenge, No. 80
12. Page 18, Daily Warm-Ups
13. Page 19, Essential Creativity, No. 96
14. Page 20, Sightreading Challenge, No. 100
15. Page 21, EE Quiz, No. 106
16. Page 22, Chromatic Scale, No. 107
17. Page 23, Sightreading Challenge, No. 115
18. Page 24, EE Quiz, No. 120
19. Page 25, EE Quiz, No. 126
20. Page 27, EE Quiz, No. 133
21. Page 30, Natural Minor Scale, No. 144
22. Page 30, Harmonic Minor Scale, No. 146
23. Page 30, Pomp and Circumstance, No. 148
24. Page 31, Performance Spotlight
25. Page 32, Performance Spotlight
26. Page 33, Performance Spotlight
27. Page 38–39, Individual Study
28. Page 40, Performance Spotlight

MUSIC — AN ESSENTIAL ELEMENT OF LIFE

KEYBOARD PERCUSSION INSTRUMENTS

Each keyboard percussion instrument has a unique sound because of the materials used to create the instrument. Ranges may differ with some models of instruments.

Instrument Care Reminders

- Cover all percussion instruments when they are not being used.
- Put mallets away in a storage area. Keep the percussion section neat!
- Mallets are the only things which should be placed on your instrument. NEVER put or allow others to put objects on any percussion instrument.

BELLS (Orchestra Bells)

- Bars - metal alloy or steel
- Mallets - lexan (hard plastic), brass or hard rubber
- Range - 2 1/2 octaves
- Sounds 2 octaves higher than written

XYLOPHONE

- Bars - wooden or synthetic
- Mallets - hard rubber
- Range - 3 1/2 octaves
- Sounds 1 octave higher than written

Instruments and photos courtesy of Yamaha.

MARIMBA

- Bars – wooden (wider than xylophone bars)
- Resonating tube located below each bar
- Mallets – soft to medium rubber or yarn covered
- Range – 4 1/3 octaves (reads bass and treble clefs)
- Sounding pitch is the same as written pitch

VIBRAPHONE

- Bars – metal alloy or aluminum
- Resonating tubes located below each bar
- Adjustable electric fans in each resonator create "vibrato" effect
- Mallets – yarn covered
- Range – 3 octaves
- Sounding pitch is the same as written pitch

CHIMES

- Bars – metal tubes
- Mallets – plastic, rawhide or wooden
- Range – 1 1/2 octaves
- Sounding pitch is the same as written pitch

Reference Index

Definitions (pg.)

Book 1 Review

Composers

World Music

Reference Index for Percussion

Definitions (pg.)

*These page numbers refer to the first section (percussion) of this book.